Secure Borders, Safe Haven:

Integration with Diversity in Modern Britain

*Presented to Parliament
by the Secretary of State for the Home Department
by Command of Her Majesty
February 2002*

CM 5387

£17.75

Foreword

by the Home Secretary, the Rt Hon David Blunkett MP

There is nothing more controversial, and yet more natural, than men and women from across the world seeking a better life for themselves and their families. Ease of communication and of transportation have transformed the time it takes to move across the globe. This ease of movement has broken down traditional boundaries. Yet the historic causes of homelessness, hunger or fear – conflict, war and persecution – have not disappeared. That is why economic migration and the seeking of asylum are as prevalent today as they have been at times of historic trauma.

But the tensions, as well as the enrichment, which flow from the inward migration of those arriving on our often wet and windy shores, must be understood, debated, and addressed. Migration is an inevitable reality of the modern world and it brings significant benefits. But to ensure that we sustain the positive contribution of migration to our social well-being and economic prosperity, we need to manage it properly and build firmer foundations on which integration with diversity can be achieved.

Confidence, security and trust make all the difference in enabling a safe haven to be offered to those coming to the UK. To enable integration to take place, and to value the diversity it brings, we need to be secure within our sense of belonging and identity and therefore to be able to reach out and to embrace those who come to the UK. Those who wish to work and to contribute to the UK, as well as those who seek to escape from persecution, will then receive the welcome they deserve.

Having a clear, workable and robust nationality and asylum system is the pre-requisite to building the security and trust that is needed. Without it, we cannot defeat those who would seek to stir up hate, intolerance and prejudice. The Government, and those agencies and organisations delivering nationality, immigration and asylum services, need to demonstrate that they know what they are doing, and that they are doing it well.

Only in this way will we be able to expose the nonsense of the claim that people coming through the Channel Tunnel, or crossing in container lorries, constitutes an invasion when it patently demonstrates how difficult people are finding it to reach this country.

Nevertheless, the fact that they are so desperate to do so raises a number of critical issues. One of these is clearly the perception that Britain is a stable and attractive place in which to settle. This view arises not simply because of our buoyant and successful economy, and the employment opportunities it has brought, but also because the universality of the English language and global communication flows mean that millions of people hear about the UK and often aspire to come here.

We should be proud that this view of the UK is held around the world. But that is quite different from the perception amongst some that we are out of line with other European nations in the way in which we deal with illegal immigration and asylum seekers.

This mistaken perception may arise in part because of the differences between the UK and the rest of Europe in respect of internal identification procedures. That is why a debate around the issue of entitlement cards is so important and why the Government wishes to present a full consultation paper, including the whole issue of identity fraud, for widespread debate in the late spring or early summer.

At the same time, we need to send out a signal around the world that we are neither open to abuse nor a 'Fortress Britain'. Our system combines rational and controlled routes for economic migration with fair, but robust, procedures for dealing with those who claim asylum.

It is possible to square the circle. It is a 'two-way street' requiring commitment and action from the host community, asylum seekers and long-term migrants alike. We have fundamental moral obligations which we will always honour. We must uphold basic human rights, tackling the racism and prejudice which people still face too often. At the same time, those coming into our country have duties that they need to understand and which facilitate their acceptance and integration.

In addition, we expect something more than the international 'free for all', the so called 'asylum shopping' throughout Europe, and the 'it is not our problem' attitude which is too often displayed. We therefore expect Europe and the developed nations across the world to respond through cooperation and reciprocation in a way that makes it possible for a nation like Britain to accept its responsibilities gladly, and to be able to manage them effectively.

In setting out a policy on citizenship, immigration and asylum it is this recognition of global movement, mass communication and the changing international situation that has to inform our thinking if we are determined to develop the type of society we all want to be part of. It means ensuring we understand and apply our obligations under international law and that we have the systems in place to operate a modern, flexible and coherent immigration policy. This means welcoming those who have a contribution to make to our country, offering refuge to those who have a well-founded fear of persecution and engaging those who seek citizenship so they can enjoy the full benefits of this status and understand the obligations that go with it.

We will need to be tough in tackling, Europe-wide, the people traffickers who use the misery of others for their own gain. It requires us to tackle illegal working, ending exploitation in the shadow economy and dealing with gangmasters and corrupt businesses who evade taxes and undercut fairness and decency for the rest of society. We need radical changes to our asylum system to ensure its effectiveness, fairness and integrity.

This White Paper sets out how we propose to develop these principles to produce a policy that looks forward and is capable of meeting the needs of the country and the individuals who come here. A policy that recognises the need to change and develop. A nationality, immigration and asylum policy that secures the sustainable growth and social inclusion that are an essential part of our core principles and the delivery targets of my Department.

Decisions on the implementation and level of resources for the proposals in this White Paper will, of course, be taken in the forthcoming Spending Review alongside decisions on the Government's other priorities.

Contents

Executive summary

1   This White Paper sets out the key challenges we face in developing our nationality, immigration and asylum policy and sets out in detail the measures we are taking to produce a coherent strategy.

2   Migration is a consistent feature of human history. But in recent years, the changes associated with globalisation have led to greater complexity in patterns of migration, and new domestic and international challenges for government and communities to address. These challenges are cultural, economic and social.

3   Migration brings huge benefits: increased skills, enhanced levels of economic activity, cultural diversity and global links. But it can also raise tensions unless properly understood and well managed. Countries offering refuge to those fleeing persecution and war, as well as accepting economic migration to meet their core economic and skills needs, need to be confident in their identity and sense of belonging, and trust their immigration and asylum systems to work fairly and effectively. Strong civic and community foundations are necessary if people are to have the confidence to welcome asylum seekers and migrants. They must trust the systems their governments operate and believe they are fair and not abused. They must have a sense of their own community or civic identity – a sense of shared understanding which can both animate and give moral content to the benefits and duties of the citizenship to which new entrants aspire. Only then can integration with diversity be achieved.

Citizenship & Nationality

4   The first challenge migration poses is to our concepts of national identity and citizenship. Migration has increased the diversity of advanced democracies, leading to changes in national culture and identity. Many of us already have overlapping identities based on our cultural and ethnic backgrounds. More than half of the countries of the world now accept dual citizenship. At the same time, globalisation of communication media and information technology has opened up national cultures to diverse influences, and provided channels of mutual interaction between different parts of the world that literally know no boundaries.

Social changes such as the decline of old certainties of class or place, and the emergence of new political institutions alongside the nation state, have also contributed to these changes in identity and political belonging.

5 All major democracies have had to face up to these changes in different ways in recent decades. In important respects, the UK has responded successfully to diversity. Unlike many other countries, British nationality has never been associated with membership of a particular ethnic group. For centuries we have been a multi-ethnic nation. We do not exclude people from citizenship on the basis of their race or ethnicity. Similarly, our society is based on cultural difference, rather than assimilation to a prevailing monoculture. This diversity is a source of pride, and it helps to explain our cultural vitality, the strength of our economy and our strong international links.

6 But, in other areas, we have failed. The reports into last summer's disturbances in Bradford, Oldham and Burnley painted a vivid picture of fractured and divided communities, lacking a sense of common values or shared civic identity to unite around. The reports signalled the need for us to foster and renew the social fabric of our communities, and rebuild a sense of common citizenship, which embraces the different and diverse experiences of today's Britain.

7 In this context, citizenship is not just for those entering the country – it is for all British citizens. Citizenship is now taught in schools as a fundamental part of the national curriculum. But we need to engage people of all ages and walks of life. The Government will initiate an open and constructive debate about citizenship, civic identity and shared values. It is only through having such a debate that we will have the basis for bringing together people of different races, cultures and religions in a cohesive society. This dialogue will form a central part of our drive for civil renewal in all our communities. Community cohesion and commonality of citizenship is weak. Too many of our citizens are excluded from meaningful participation in society. This is true of those in white working class communities whose alienation from the political process, along with their physical living conditions and standards of living, leaves them feeling excluded from the increased wealth and improved quality of life which they see around them. In the same way, those who have entered this country and joined friends, family or ethnic groupings may find themselves experiencing relative economic disadvantage and sometimes overt racism.

8 In this White Paper, the Government sets out our key objectives for the development of citizenship and nationality policy. To ensure social integration and cohesion in the UK, we need to develop a stronger understanding of what citizenship really means. Historically, the UK has had a relatively weak sense of what active citizenship should entail. Our values of individual

freedom, the protection of liberty and respect for difference, have not been accompanied by a strong, shared understanding of the civic realm. The acquisition of British nationality is a bureaucratic exercise, with almost no effort made to engage new members of the community with the fundamentals of our democracy and society.

9   In an increasingly diverse world, it is vital that we strengthen both our sense of community belonging and the civic and political dimensions of British citizenship. In particular, we intend to offer language teaching and light touch education for citizenship for those making a home in the UK – with a view to a simple examination for citizenship applicants similar to that which exists in many other countries. This will strengthen the ability of new citizens to participate in society and to engage actively in our democracy. This will help people understand both their rights and their obligations as citizens of the UK, and strengthen the bonds of mutual understanding between people of diverse cultural backgrounds. It will also help to promote individuals' economic and social integration. We have no wish to see applicants fail the requirements. We want to see them meet the requirements and become British citizens. If they do fail, they can apply again whenever they wish.

10   Chapter 2 sets out how we will promote the importance of British naturalisation by:

- Speeding up the process of obtaining citizenship.
- Preparing people for citizenship by promoting language training and education for citizenship.
- Celebrating the acquisition of citizenship by introducing citizenship ceremonies.
- Updating our deprivation of citizenship procedures.
- Reforming our nationality legislation.

Working in the UK

11   The second challenge is economic: what does the UK need to do to ensure that it has the people it needs to prosper in the world economy? And how can we open up opportunities that allow people who want to work here, and can contribute to our society, to do so without attempting to enter using illegal routes? Alongside increasing flows of people, developed economies are becoming more knowledge-based and more dependent on people with skills and ideas. Migrants bring new experiences and talents that can widen and enrich the knowledge base of the economy. Human skills and ambitions have become the building blocks of successful economies and the self-selection of migrants means they are likely to bring valuable ideas, entrepreneurship, ambition and energy.

12   We have taken steps to ensure that people with the skills and talents we need are able to come into the UK on a sensible and managed basis. Following the review conducted in 2000, we have made significant improvements to the work permit system, both in terms of policy and the way the service is delivered. For example, we have simplified the eligibility criteria, introduced the facility to submit applications electronically and achieved substantial reductions in turnaround times. Until January 2001, 70% of complete applications were decided within one week of receipt. Now the standard is 90% of complete applications decided within one day of receipt. The service is highly regarded by employers who use it. In September 2000 we also introduced a new way for people to enter through the Innovator Scheme which allows entrepreneurs with business plans that can generate significant benefits for the UK to enter and set up businesses. We estimate that each individual entering through this Scheme will create an additional 10 jobs for UK workers.

13   This is not an alternative to developing the skills base and productivity of those already resident. Our priority will remain investment in the skills and abilities of the existing population. But migration, carefully managed to meet particular needs within a particular sector or at a particular skill level, can help to support these policies as we engage the entrepreneurship, drive and enterprise of those who have sought to make the UK their home. It is, however, in those communities least likely to have benefited from added value economic activity and entrepreneurship where the biggest challenge lies. For even at a time of high levels of economic activity and buoyant employment, the low skill or no skill groupings are likely to be most fearful of the low skill, no skill entrant into the local economy. But research suggests that migrants do not compete for jobs with existing workers. The idea that there are only a fixed number of jobs in the economy has been discredited. Migrants can also expand sectors, create new businesses and jobs, thereby increasing production and employment opportunities for existing workers. Migration can also bring benefits for source developing countries, in particular through remittance flows and returning migrants applying enhanced skills and knowledge. The Home Office will work closely with other Departments, particularly the Department for Work and Pensions, the Department for Education and Skills and the Department for International Development, to ensure that our migration policies complement other policies for the labour market, integration and international development.

14   Chapter 3 sets out how we are enhancing the current routes of entry and tightening procedures through:

- The introduction of a Highly Skilled Migrant Programme to enable the most talented migrants to work in the UK.
- Changing the Immigration Rules to let certain postgraduate students switch into employment.

- Meeting the demand for short-term casual labour building on the principles of the Seasonal Agricultural Workers' Scheme.

- Publishing a consultation document about the Working Holidaymaker Scheme to take views on ensuring the scheme is as inclusive as possible.

- Ensuring Ministers of religion are suitably qualified to fulfil their role for the benefit of the community.

- Regulation of those who provide advice and services regarding work permit applications.

Asylum Policy: Ensuring End-to-End Credibility

15   Disentangling the many motives – from seeking better economic prospects to seeking protection – which people have for coming to the UK is not always easy. But we need to do more to ensure that clear, managed routes into the UK exist so that people do not use inappropriate routes to effect their entry. In particular, we must ensure that the asylum system is returned to what it was always intended to be – a system for those who are in need of protection and for whom protection cannot be delivered through alternative means. The measures set out in this White Paper will help to achieve this. More legitimate routes are being created for those with work-related motives to apply for entry to the UK; and as we provide gateways through a resettlement programme, we will be reducing the justification for those with protection needs to travel long distances before seeking protection. Over half of people who apply for asylum are currently found not to be in need of any form of international protection. It is this misuse of the asylum procedures that creates so many of the difficulties and costs in operating an effective system. By increasing the legal routes for entering the UK there will be fewer reasons for unfounded asylum claimants to use the asylum route. That will be a benefit to everyone, especially those who are refugees.

16   We have made substantial improvements to our asylum system in recent years. As a result of our 1998 White Paper 'Fairer, Faster and Firmer – A Modern Approach to Immigration and Asylum'[1], and the Immigration and Asylum Act 1999 that followed it, the system has improved considerably:

- Delay and backlogs in the system have been reduced.
- A National Asylum Support Service has been introduced.
- Oakington Reception Centre has been set up to decide straightforward asylum claims in about 7-10 days.

[1] The Home Office, London: The Stationery Office 1998.

- An electronic fingerprint system has been introduced to deter multiple applications and improve identification procedures.
- Immigration enforcement powers have been strengthened.
- Resources are better targeted through an intelligence-led approach.
- Statutory regulation of immigration advisers has been introduced to deal with unscrupulous advisers who assist fraudulent claims and exploit their clients.
- A one-stop appeals system has been introduced.

17   However, the scale and pace of change in the external environment requires us to undertake further radical reform. And it is clear that many parts of the system are not working effectively. It must be quicker and less open to fraud. The key principles underpinning our reforms are that asylum seekers are both supported and tracked though the system in a process of induction, accommodation and reporting and fast-track removal or integration.

18   We have said that we need radical changes to our asylum system to ensure its effectiveness, fairness and integrity. Creating a coherent overall immigration strategy, through the expansion of entry routes described above, is an essential element to this. But within that framework, we also need changes to the asylum system itself to make it work for the benefit of all. Underlying these changes are the following key points:

- The ultimate aims of the asylum system are to determine who is and is not in need of protection. Providing a safe haven and integrating quickly into UK society those who are in need of such protection and to remove quickly those who are not.
- Everyone who applies for asylum can expect – and will be given – a clear outline of the procedures that will apply to them.
- Everyone will be subjected to a more managed system so that we can keep in contact with them throughout the process. They will be expected to co-operate fully in complying with that system and in providing information related to their claim. If they do not do so, it will adversely affect the credibility of their claim for asylum and increase the chances of their claim being refused.
- The legislative structure will be simplified, to make things clearer. All adult applicants who enter the UK's asylum system will have their claims considered under the same basic legal framework, and be covered by the new managed regime. Provision to deal more quickly at the application and appeal stages will remain – for example, to give priority to cases which appear to be straightforward grants or refusals, or where a person is not complying with the new regime.

- When someone has been through the system and has been successful, they can expect to be given quick and effective help to aid their integration into UK society. And removing the scope for delaying tactics will lead to the early identification of those not in need of protection and who are expected to return to their own country; and the ability to enforce the removal of any such person who declines to leave voluntarily.

19   Such a system will be one which is truly 'end-to-end' in its approach. It will be a quick, high-quality, highly-managed system, which will assist those in genuine need of protection. And enable us to return swiftly those not in need of protection. That will greatly enhance the integrity of the asylum system.

20   The Government's policy of dispersing asylum seekers is designed to ensure that the burden on services is shared across the country, and not borne overwhelmingly in London and the South East. This principle will be upheld as new trial Accommodation Centres are developed. However, in developing these, we have, as set out in the review published on 29 October last year, acknowledged that the dispersal system is in need of substantial improvement. Accommodation Centres, providing facilities on site, will help to ensure that dispersal does not cause problems for the local neighbourhood and help with the process of acceptance. But asylum seekers are only part of the equation: we must do more to understand overall migration patterns and the impact they have on services in different parts of the country.

21   Chapter 4 sets out how we will fundamentally reform the asylum system. We will do this by:

- Preparing a resettlement programme with the UNHCR, establishing gateways for those most in need of protection to come here legally.
- Introducing a managed system of induction, accommodation, reporting and removal centres to secure a seamless asylum process.
- The introduction of an Application Registration Card to provide more secure and certain evidence of identity and nationality.
- Phasing out voucher support.
- Better assisting unaccompanied asylum seeking children and sharing support for these children across a wider number of local authorities while sifting out adults posing as children.
- Streamlining our appeals system to minimise delay and helping to cut down barriers to removal.
- Developing a strategy to increase the number of removals of people who have no claim to stay here.
- Enhancing the opportunities for those accepted as refugees to play a full role in society through our Refugee Integration Programme and active labour market measures.

Tackling Fraud – People Trafficking, Illegal Entry and Illegal Working

22   At the heart of our challenges lie those who will take advantage of global movements to traffic or smuggle migrants. Organised immigration crime is a growth industry, worth millions of pounds each year. It is, by its nature, an area where reliable information is scarce, but our research and intelligence on it have been improving. While some of it is perpetrated by small scale opportunists, there is evidence that it is becoming the preserve of increasingly sophisticated organised groups, some concentrating on either people smuggling or exploitation, others covering both. It appears that established criminal networks are moving in, including those already smuggling drugs. Their aim has been to cash in on global increases in migration flows. They hope to use the smuggling infrastructure and know-how they have developed, while avoiding the increasingly effective prosecution and tough penalties for drug trafficking. There is also increasing intelligence linking trafficking and smuggling groups with crimes of violence, highlighting the often brutal nature of the trade.

23   We need to strengthen the law by increasing penalties and taking advantage of new technology to identify illegal entrants before they establish themselves here. And we will continue to develop preventative projects to tackle the problem at source and seek to reduce the vulnerability of those who are trafficked. Co-operation is the key between agencies in the UK and within Europe. Immigration crime is international and we must think in these terms if we are to succeed.

24   A properly managed system needs to adopt a broad approach, recognising that the system works as a whole with movement and flexibility between routes. It has to close the gaps for illegal entry, illegal working and abuse of the system. Irregular migration undermines the integrity of the system. It profits traffickers, smugglers and unscrupulous employers, damages legitimate business, makes illegal migrant workers vulnerable to exploitation and social exclusion, and may be costly through lost revenue from taxation and National Insurance contributions.

25   To tackle illegal migrant working we must address the causes. Alongside our policies to improve the efficiency of the labour market, the development of managed migration schemes will help to ensure that, wherever possible, those wishing to come to the UK have legal routes open for them to do so and employers can fill vacancies with legal workers. We will take tough action on employers who employ illegal workers and on people traffickers and smugglers. We will confiscate the proceeds of crime so that traffickers and employers who break the law do not benefit from illegal migration. These measures will send out a clear message to illegal workers and their employers.

26   In tandem with an efficient, well-managed asylum system and sensible controlled avenues of legal employment we will reduce the opportunities and incentives for the criminals.

27   Chapter 5 explains the measures we are taking. We will:

- Combat illegal working through improved enforcement action, less potential for fraud, effective gathering and sharing of information and working with business and the trades unions.
- Strengthen the law, including a 14 year penalty for facilitating illegal entry and trafficking for the purposes of sexual exploitation.
- Deal appropriately and compassionately with victims of trafficking, offering new forms of help to those trapped in conditions of gross exploitation.
- Target the criminals through intelligence and enforcement operations.
- Co-operate extensively with EU and other international partners.
- Tackle organised crime through prevention strategies in source and transit countries.

Border controls

28   The challenge here is to allow those who qualify for entry to pass through the controls as quickly as possible, maximising the time spent on identifying those who try to enter clandestinely or by presenting forged or stolen documents. Increasingly we are looking at new methods of detecting and deterring. We must continue to develop in response to the changing methods and routes of entry. Our network of Airline Liaison Officers enables practical support to be given to airlines to help them identify fraudulent documents. Pre-clearance in the Czech Republic and enabling UK immigration officers to conduct passport checks in France are further examples of how we are engaging positively in the European and international arena to disrupt the flows of those who do not qualify. While the growth of telecommunications allows the traffickers to exchange information, technology offers us the chance to gain greater control through the use of scanners to detect those hidden in vehicles.

29   We will continue to think flexibly to identify ways of speeding up the admission of frequent passengers and those who have already been accepted to travel here. The less time the Immigration Service needs to spend on clearing passengers, the more they can concentrate on those who seek to undermine our laws. The Government is proposing to extend automation of entry processes and to examine whether an authority to carry could be granted to the carrier at the time a person books their ticket.

30   Chapter 6 explains what we are doing to protect our borders and speed up procedures for genuine passengers. We are:

- Deploying Airline Liaison Officers overseas to help prevent improperly documented passengers travelling to the UK.
- Using visa regimes for nationals of countries where there is evidence of systematic abuse of our controls.
- Placing immigration officers abroad where this is necessary to check passengers before they travel to the UK.
- Maintaining our operational arrangements for UK immigration officers to conduct passport checks in France.
- Developing a new concept of screening passengers before they travel to the UK.
- Using technology such as iris or facial recognition and fingerprints for the improved control and security of passengers.
- Utilising x/gamma ray scanners, CCTV and other new technology to help locate those seeking to enter illegally.
- Using mobile task forces as part of an intelligence-led control.
- Working with European partners and others to strengthen the EU's common borders and enhance border controls on transit routes.

Marriages and family visits

31   With the increase in international trade and more UK citizens working abroad, it is not surprising that there is an increase in the numbers of British citizens marrying foreign nationals. In addition, there has been a tradition of families originating from the Indian sub-continent wanting to bring spouses from arranged marriages to live with them in the UK. In 2000, over 38,000 people were granted settlement on the basis of marriage.

32   The majority of those seeking leave to remain on the basis of marriage have entered into genuine relationships and intend to live permanently with their spouse. But we know that large profits and financial rewards can be obtained as a result of arranging bogus or sham marriages. We want to make it more difficult for those who seek to stay on the basis of a bogus marriage while simplifying procedures where there is clear evidence that a genuine marriage exists. Alongside this we will recognise changes in marital trends. We also believe there is a discussion to be had within those communities that continue the practice of arranged marriages as to whether more of these could be undertaken within the settled community here.

33   We will also continue our efforts to find the best way for family members to come to the UK for events such as weddings or funerals. We know the anguish that is caused where applications are refused. We need to demonstrate that the system works effectively to allow fast and efficient service for those who have a genuine need to come to the UK at a certain time while ensuring there is no abuse of our procedures.

34   Chapter 7 sets out how we will take forward measures. We will:

- Increase the probationary period for leave to remain on the basis of marriage.
- Revise the Immigration Rules for unmarried partners.
- Simplify the procedures for legitimate applicants.
- Consider revising the Immigration Rules to prevent switching into marriage for people entering the UK for 6 months or less.
- Publish the results of a detailed review about rights of appeal in family visit cases and use this consultation to examine what further work is necessary to improve our systems.

War criminals

35   Many asylum seekers come to the UK seeking protection from conflict or war in their own country. Where large numbers of people are fleeing abroad for their own safety, it is easy for individuals who have been involved in the commission of war crimes or crimes against humanity to travel – perhaps under an assumed identity or without documents – to the safety of another country unchecked, seeking asylum on arrival.

36   Recent conflict in the Balkans, Rwanda and Afghanistan demonstrates that many people will seek protection in the UK. The Government is committed to fulfilling its international obligations to protect those in genuine need but it is equally committed to ensuring that those who have been involved in the commission of war crimes and crimes against humanity are not able to abuse the hospitality of the UK.

37   So Chapter 7 also focuses on how we will strengthen our ability to deal with war criminals. We will:

- Strengthen relevant immigration and nationality legislation.
- Ensure better co-ordination amongst Departments and agencies.

Summary

38   This White Paper sets out a package of measures to meet the opportunities and challenges that face us now and will do so in the future. The objectives are clear. We will develop our citizenship and nationality policy to create a supportive, safe and cohesive community. We will manage flows through legitimate entry routes, developing managed migration policies to attract the people we need to compete and prosper in the global economy in a manner consistent with our international commitment to eliminate world poverty and domestic commitment to achieve employment opportunities for all. We will develop our methods to counteract organised immigration crime and illegal working and crack down on those who undermine and abuse our system. And fundamental to our moral and humanitarian objectives we will develop a seamless asylum process which is clear from induction to integration or return.

39   Together these measures will fundamentally reform our citizenship, asylum and immigration system presenting a rational approach to the global movements of the 21st century.

Consultation

The Government would welcome comments on the proposals in this White Paper.

These should be sent by **21 March 2002** to:

>   White Paper Comments
>   The New Policy Team
>   Immigration and Nationality Directorate
>   6th Floor
>   Apollo House
>   Croydon CR9 3RR

Or by fax to: 020 8760 8008

Or by e-mail to: IND.NPT.Whitepapercomments@homeoffice.gsi.gov.uk

**The Government may be asked to publish responses to this White Paper. Please let us know
if you do not want your comments to be published.**

Chapter 1

INTRODUCTION AND OVERVIEW

Managing the different migration flows

1.1   One of the issues which troubles the public most in relation to nationality and immigration is a belief that entry into this country and residence here is subject to abuse. The amount of column inches devoted to those trying to reach our shores through clandestine routes illustrates that the issue of asylum outweighs the much broader debate about migration, nationality and integration.

1.2   This White Paper intends to refocus the agenda onto the wider issues of migration: on the global reality of increasing international mobility, how we can harness the benefits of this movement for all concerned (sending and receiving countries), and how we can foster a greater sense of community and social integration at home.

1.3   If managed properly, migration can bring considerable benefits to the UK, including improvements in economic growth and productivity, as well as cultural enrichment and diversity. 'Managing' migration means having an orderly, organised, and enforceable system of entry. It also means managing post-entry integration and inclusion in the economy and society, helping migrants to find their feet, and enabling members of the existing population to welcome them into their communities.

1.4   At present our main routes of entry are for work-related or humanitarian purposes. But there are many different, and diverse, reasons why people may decide to move to another country, stay there (and for how long), return home, or move on to a third country, and a range of ways and means by which they gain entry to the UK. It is essential to have a coherent overview of the whole system.

1.5   Where entry is not possible without taking clandestine action, a problem is clearly created which then reinforces the perception of confusion or worse – that the system is out of control. To get the balance right we need to ensure that there are managed and credible routes for men and women to reach these shores, and gain legitimate status as residents in our country, in a manner which builds confidence and reassurance.

1.6   Acceptable routes for entry and competently administered procedures, including monitoring and control, are therefore a prerequisite to getting the situation back into balance. So too are measures to tackle the issues of illegal presence and illegal working.

1.7   This White Paper sets out new proposals for managing flows of people from entry into the UK through work-related routes or the asylum system, to settlement and the acquisition of citizenship. In order to manage entry into the UK better, we are developing legal, sensible and controlled routes for economic migration; ensuring that our asylum system is fair but robust and credible; and taking the powers that we need to tackle the criminals who abuse our borders and exploit desperate people. In order to improve post-entry inclusion and planning for the future we are developing our principles of, and policies on, citizenship and nationality and integration.

1.8   The next two sections of this Chapter set out the context and constraints within which migration policy must be viewed: the challenges of globalisation, and the challenges at home. We must be realistic about, and responsive to, our global environment. We must also be focused on our domestic environment and committed to continuing to promote community cohesion and social integration at home.

The challenge of globalisation

1.9   Globalisation is bringing rapid changes to the world in which we live. Over the last quarter of the century, a series of economic, technological and social changes have increased the interdependence and interconnectedness of the modern world. International trade and transnational movements in capital have grown exponentially as transport and transaction costs have fallen and barriers to mobility have come down. Advances in technology have revolutionised communications and the mass media, opening up instantaneous exchange of information and knowledge at the press of a button.

1.10   These changes have had profound consequences for the movement of people. They are now increasingly able to move around the world, whether to work, travel or seek refuge. Migration flows have accelerated and become more complex, whilst increasing global trade in services and expansion of leisure travel have vastly increased the numbers of people crossing national borders. New forms of migration have emerged and networks have sprung up to facilitate this movement. Further liberalisation of the movement of persons for the delivery of services is currently under negotiation in the World Trade Organisation under the General Agreement on Trade in Services. These negotiations offer an opportunity to establish fair and clear regulations governing temporary movement of workers which do not unnecessarily restrict trade in services and bring benefits to both developed and developing countries. For example, they could facilitate movement such as that of employees of transnationals moving temporarily from country to country. At the other end of the spectrum, criminal gangs smuggle and traffic people across continents, exploiting their desperation to escape war, persecution or poverty. Migration to the UK is only one small part of these global movements of people. We need a more sophisticated understanding of the drivers of migration and asylum seeking, and the networks that facilitate these movements, so that we can harness their benefits and also tackle detrimental criminal and trafficking activities.

1.11   Globally, the number of international migrants increased from 75 million to 120 million between 1965 and 1990[2]. By 2000 168 million people were living outside their country of birth, an increase in the proportion of migrants to 2.8%. Of these, the United Nations High Commissioner for Refugees estimates that 12 million are refugees, and a further 9 million are stateless or displaced persons, recent returnees and others of concern.

1.12   The number of people coming to the UK each year has risen substantially over the past decade. In 1990, there were around 50 million arrivals at UK ports. By 2000, this had risen to almost 90 million. Around 86% of these were British citizens returning from abroad and European Economic Area (EEA) nationals but there were also 13 million arrivals from outside the EEA. The vast majority of these were visitors coming to the UK on holiday or business who subsequently returned to their own country but around 600,000 came to the UK for other reasons (as students, to work or as family dependants). In some areas there has been considerable movement. In 2001, for instance, 104,000 new work permits were issued (work permits and first permissions), the highest number ever and significantly more than the 80,000 new work permits issued in 2000.

1.13   One of the key drivers for more people coming to the UK is our strong economic position. In terms of international trade and investment, the UK is a relatively open economy. This puts the UK in a good position to take advantage of increasing global trade and to benefit rapidly from new developments, ideas and production techniques. The UK has a higher level of employment and lower level of unemployment than virtually every other country in the European Union (EU). Our strong labour market acts as a magnet for those seeking better jobs and lives for themselves and their families. In addition, EU nationals have the right under EC law to live and work in the UK and in 2000 over a quarter of the foreign-born migrants were citizens of other EU countries. The expansion of EU membership will further increase the number of people with the right to live and work in the UK.

2   Population Division of the United Nations Secretariat, 'Trends in total migrant stock by sex' Revision 4, 1998.

Table 1: Non-EEA nationals given entry to the UK

Number of journeys

Purpose of journey	1995	2000
Students	285,000	313,000
WP holders for more than 12 months	11,700	36,300
WP holders for less than 12 months	26,100	30,800
Agricultural Workers	4,660	10,100
Working Holidaymakers	36,000	38,500
UK grandparent ancestry	6,620	11,000
Domestic employee	11,800	14,300
Au Pair	11,700	12,900
Investors	10	50
Family Reunion and other dependants	48,400	74,200
Accepted for settlement on arrival	2,400	2,290
Asylum seekers and their dependents	3,700	11,400
Others	51,200	48,000
Total	499,290	602,840

Source: Home Office.

1.14 The flow of people into the UK tells only part of the story. Patterns of movement show that migration is not a one way, one off process and that the UK may be used as a stepping stone to other countries. There are a whole range of reasons why people may decide to leave their home countries, settle abroad, return to their own country of origin or move on to a new destination. In 2000 almost 300,000 people left the UK compared with 480,000 coming in. Some of these will be British citizens emigrating but others will be migrants returning home or moving to other countries.

1.15 The expansion of migration is unlikely to diminish in the future. In the next 25 years, the world's population is expected to grow by a further 2 billion, 98% of whom will be in developing countries. This growth will be accompanied by an ageing of the population in OECD countries, intensifying pressures to migrate from low-income countries experiencing increased competition for jobs and scarce resources to countries like the UK experiencing a shrinking in the number of people of working age. With birth rates continuing to fall in the UK, net inward migration has become the biggest component of population change. In 2000, foreign-born migrants constituted nearly 8 per cent of the total UK population.

1.16 Globalisation also means that issues previously considered 'domestic' are now increasingly international. When people and ideas cross borders, Government policymaking must respond, anticipate new challenges and be ready to capitalise on the benefits. Globalisation means that what happens in the UK must be considered in the wider European and international context, since no single country can frame its response to the global environment in isolation from others. The breadth of causes and consequences of migration mean that migration policies across countries must be integrated and reflect the impact on the countries concerned.

1.17   Migration and asylum issues cut across economic, social, foreign and international development policy boundaries. We need to bring order to the disparate flows of people by developing legal routes of entry for those who will benefit our economy and those who need our protection. The traffickers thrive on disorder and disharmony. Where there is a demand they will seek to meet it and where there are differences they will exploit them. It has never been more important for us to work in partnership with our European colleagues to secure a system which separates the initial flight from persecution from subsequent migratory movement. Minimum standards and common interpretations of the laws are crucial elements in bringing about this management of human flows.

1.18   Reflecting the growing awareness of the need to co-ordinate immigration matters, the European Commission has introduced a number of Directives with regard to the entry and stay of third country nationals in the European Union covering employment, family reunification and long-term residence. We have made clear that we will maintain the UK's system of frontier controls and nothing being developed or negotiated in Europe will undermine this. But we also need to involve ourselves actively in considering the implications and effects of this work. The Government will continue to give careful consideration to the future exercise of our right to opt into EU measures on immigration and asylum, considering the need for, and benefits of, effective co-operation while preserving our frontier controls.

1.19   We must also ensure that our immigration policies are consistent with our fundamental commitment to eliminate world poverty. Migration flows can be highly beneficial to developing countries: remittances from migrant workers make a major contribution to many economies; extensive trade links are forged; and skills and knowledge shared. The Government will seek to ensure that developing countries are able to integrate into, and benefit from, the global economy. This will involve increased movement in persons and global trade in services.

1.20   But, at the same time, the increase in international competition for people with scarce skills means that we need to ensure that measures aimed at meeting the demands for skills in the UK economy are not at the expense of the growth and development of poor countries. We will fulfil the commitment in the White Paper, *'Eliminating World Poverty: Making Globalisation Work for the Poor* [3] *'* that the UK will ensure migration policies do not worsen

3   Department for International Development, London: The Stationery Office, 2000.

skills shortages in developing countries. We will seek to develop innovative approaches for use in sectors identified by developing countries as potentially vulnerable to a skills drain. These will build on the experience of the Code of Practice used by the Department of Health to limit the skills drain caused by active recruitment of health workers from developing countries and we will monitor and ensure compliance with such measures.

The challenges at home

1.21   If we are to maintain and develop social cohesion and harmony within the United Kingdom it is crucial that we make sense of these global flows. Our domestic and social policies in relation to nationality, immigration and asylum applications must therefore respond both to the reality beyond our borders and the danger posed by well meaning but indecisive drift at home.

1.22   This is why the Home Secretary's statement of 29 October 2001 set out a new framework and set of administrative processes to tackle immediate problems. This White Paper expands on the statement and picks up on the medium and long-term challenges that face us. If we are to overcome fear, suspicion and either misunderstanding or deliberate exaggeration of the facts, it is crucial that people feel secure within their own community, and that those seeking to settle here develop a sense of belonging, an identity and shared mutual understanding, which can be passed from one generation to another. In this way we will break down the intolerance and prejudice which is so destructive to social cohesion.

1.23   This means that we need to be sensitive to the potential problems as well as being quick to harness the benefits that increasing international mobility offers. Migration can bring considerable benefits for the domestic population. Migrants can contribute to the UK by increasing economic growth, paying taxes, setting up new businesses, contributing to the expansion of new business sectors, consumer choice, and creating new jobs. But migration flows need to be properly managed in order to achieve these benefits and to ensure that they are consistent with all our aims and objectives for individuals, businesses and the public sector.

1.24   We will be careful to consider the impact on existing workers, especially on the most disadvantaged groups, when developing routes of entry. There may be concerns that migration has a negative effect on the job or training opportunities for the existing population, although the research in the UK finds little indication of a negative impact on employment. If anything, it suggests a positive effect on the wage levels. The Home Office has funded several studies on the impact and outcomes of migration in the UK over the last 12 months. The findings are heavily constrained by the limitations of the data on migrant outcomes in the UK but are consistent with the view that migrants help ease recruitment difficulties and expand sectors, thereby increasing the productivity of the existing population. They support similar research undertaken abroad. A recent study of labour mobility in Europe by PricewaterhouseCoopers[4], which involved interviews with individuals and businesses, found that the most common response to recruitment difficulties was to undertake training (nearly 50% of firms included this in their strategy for dealing with recruitment difficulties), followed by using new technology, and improving pay and benefits (a particularly common answer amongst UK firms).

1.25   We need to address the local level impacts of migration which may contribute to local community tensions. A crucial element of our vision for migration reform is the strengthening of community cohesion and social integration. Strong, cohesive and confident communities are the building blocks of a healthy society. We need to develop nationality, citizenship and integration policy. We also need to ensure that we properly anticipate, plan for and fund the consequences of migration for education, health, housing and transport providers. We are working closely across all the different departments concerned, and with the devolved administrations, to ensure that these impacts are properly taken into account in planning ahead for local service provision.

1.26   We must plan for the future. Failure to ensure the successful integration of those settling in the UK today will store up problems for future generations. Sharp differences in the relative prosperity of recently settled ethnic minority communities are already becoming apparent. Our objective is to secure social cohesion and equality of opportunity between communities.

1.27   The balanced approach that we intend to develop as a consequence of adopting the policies in this White Paper will seek to provide trust, confidence, reassurance and understanding within our community. At the same time, it will offer rational, safe and workable routes for those who legitimately wish to be here. From tougher protection of our national borders to the new gateway for those seeking asylum from outside the country, we are determined to establish a system that works. This is why the new seamless approach to the administration of those claiming refugee status and the revitalisation and expansion of routes for those seeking economic migrant status go hand in hand.

---

4   PricewaterhouseCoopers, 'Mobility Matters: A European perspective'

Chapter 2

CITIZENSHIP AND NATIONALITY

2.1   The Government attaches great importance to helping those who settle here gain a fuller appreciation of the civic and political dimensions of British citizenship and, in particular, to understand the rights and responsibilities that come with the acquisition of British citizenship. This will help to strengthen active participation in the democratic process and a sense of belonging to a wider community. We believe that one means of promoting this understanding is to place much greater emphasis than we do at present on the value and significance of becoming a British citizen.

> The word 'citizenship' has been used in the context of our nationality legislation since the British Nationality Act 1948 first as 'British subject: citizenship of the UK and Colonies' and then in the British Nationality Act 1981 as 'British citizenship'. Citizenship in this context already embraces allegiance to the Sovereign and applicants for naturalisation as British citizens swear or affirm loyalty to The Queen. Although we have historically used the term 'British subjects', this status is now quite narrowly defined in our legislation and is limited to small groups of people who have links with pre-1949 Ireland and the Indian sub-continent as well as informal reference to those living here. So, in promoting citizenship in the manner described in this White Paper, we are building on an existing legal definition in a way that is fully consistent with our position as subjects of a constitutional Sovereign. There is no contradiction in promoting citizenship so that people uphold common values and understand how they can play their part in our society while upholding our status as subjects of HM The Queen.

2.2   Common citizenship is not about cultural uniformity, nor is it born out of some narrow and out-dated view of what it means to be 'British'. The Government welcomes the richness of the cultural diversity which immigrants have brought to the UK – our society is multi-cultural, and is shaped by its diverse peoples. We want British citizenship positively to embrace the diversity of background, culture and faiths that is one of the hallmarks of Britain in the 21st Century.

2.3   The Human Rights Act 1998 can be viewed as a key source of values that British citizens should share. The laws, rules and practices which govern our democracy uphold our commitment to the equal worth and dignity of all our citizens. It will sometimes be necessary to confront some cultural practices which conflict with these basic values – such as those which deny women the right to participate as equal citizens. Similarly, it means ensuring that every individual has the wherewithal, such as the ability to speak our common language, to enable them to engage as active citizens in economic, social and political life. And it means tackling racism, discrimination and prejudice wherever we find it.

2.4   The Government recognises too that, in an increasingly mobile world, more and more people will acquire more than one citizenship. The UK has long accepted the concept of dual nationality. People are not forced to give up their original citizenship in order to become British. We recognise that people will often retain a strong affinity with their country of origin. As the 1998 White Paper put it, 'it is therefore possible to be a citizen of two countries and a good citizen of both'. However, the country of main residence can and should expect every individual to be committed to accepting their responsibilities as well as embracing the rights which citizenship confers. We have introduced from this year in England compulsory teaching of citizenship and democracy in our schools and the promotion of active citizenship. This reinforces the fact that our sense of identity, understanding of our mutuality and interdependence, comes as much from the contribution we make to the world around us as it does from any theoretical entitlements we possess.

2.5   The Government also recognises that some people who may want to acquire British citizenship may find it difficult to do so because the country from which they come has a different approach to dual nationality which may, for example, impact on their nationals' property rights if they acquire a second nationality.

2.6   So, the Government's view is that we must make everyone who is settled here feel welcome and valued irrespective of whether they have acquired British citizenship. But it also believes that becoming a British citizen is a significant step which should mean more than simply obtaining the right to a British passport. The tangible benefits of becoming a British citizen will vary, depending on an individual's previous status. Importantly British citizenship confers full political rights – in particular, the right for those who do not already have it, to vote in national and European elections and the opportunity of standing for election. Whatever the specific benefits, British citizenship should bring with it a heightened commitment to full participation in British society and a recognition of the part which new citizens can play in contributing to social cohesion.

2.7 The Government believes we should do much more to prepare people for British citizenship, to enhance its significance and to celebrate its acquisition. Prior to the conferring of citizenship through naturalisation, we believe it is necessary for all those who are seeking long term resident status to be provided with the opportunity (where they do not already have the facility) to receive language training and to receive an easy to understand and practical guide in the form of both print and video, about Britain and its institutions relevant to an understanding of the society they are entering. For those moving towards naturalisation, the facility would need to be more structured as indicated below. For those simply living in our country, it is important that in the early stages after taking up residence, such support is readily available, including the immediate period after the granting of refugee status.

2.8 We will promote the importance of British citizenship by:

- Speeding up the process of acquisition.
- Preparing people for citizenship by promoting language training and education for citizenship.
- Celebrating the acquisition of citizenship.
- Updating our deprivation of citizenship procedures.
- Reforming nationality legislation.

Speeding up the process

2.9 The process of acquiring British citizenship has been taking far too long. At the end of December 1999 the average time for applicants to hear the results of their applications was nearly 20 months. The Government is committed to speeding up the process. By 31 March 2001 the waiting time had fallen to 11.6 months.

2.10 In particular, the former system of 'queuing' has been changed and since April 2001 new applications have been started on receipt. By the end of this year we anticipate all caseworkers will be considering applications on receipt leading to a further dramatic drop in the average waiting times. Applicants are also now asked to send with their applications the documents that are needed to support them, eliminating one of the causes of delay. All the applications that were in the queue when the new procedures began should have been completed by the end of December 2002. By April 2004 the average waiting time for citizenship applications should have been reduced to three months.

Figure 1: Applications for British citizenship received and decided 1990-2000

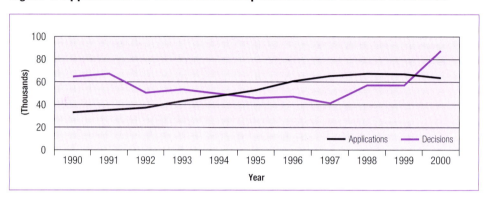

Preparing people for citizenship

2.11   Becoming British through registration or naturalisation is – or should be – a significant life event. It can be seen as an act of commitment to Britain and an important step in the process of achieving integration into our society. Yet, in spite of this, some applicants for naturalisation do not have much practical knowledge about British life or language, possibly leaving them vulnerable and ill-equipped to take an active role in society. This can lead to social exclusion and may contribute to problems of polarisation between communities. We need to develop a sense of civic identity and shared values, and knowledge of the English language (or Welsh language or Scottish Gaelic, which are provided for in the British Nationality Act 1981), can undoubtedly support this objective.

2.12   It is not altogether surprising that many applicants do not appear to attach great importance to acquiring British citizenship, beyond the convenience of obtaining a British passport. We do not actively encourage people to become British citizens or prepare them in any way. Nor, unlike some other nations, do we celebrate the acquisition of citizenship. Instead, we treat it as essentially a bureaucratic process, with a certificate being sent through the post at the end of it.

2.13   It is a fundamental objective of the Government that those living permanently in the UK should be able, through adequate command of the language and an appreciation of our democratic processes, to take their place fully in society. Evidence suggests that migrants who are fluent in English are, on average, 20 per cent more likely to be employed than those lacking fluency[5]. There is already a requirement in the British Nationality Act 1981 that applicants for naturalisation should have a sufficient command of a recognised British language but

5   'Wheatley Price and Shields, ongoing Home Office research on migrants' labour market effects

this is not really enforced in practice. It is simply assumed, unless there is evidence to the contrary. The administration of language tests as part of the naturalisation process exists in a number of countries including France, Germany, Australia and Canada. A summary of naturalisation procedures in a selection of countries is provided in Annex A.

2.14   In order to promote both the importance of an adequate command of English (or one of the recognised languages) and an understanding of British society, the Government intends to require applicants for naturalisation to demonstrate that they have achieved a certain standard. We envisage that, subject to certain limited exceptions, applicants would need to produce certificates showing that they had passed a test, if necessary after taking part in a suitable course.

2.15   Courses in English for speakers of other languages (ESOL) are already available, free of charge to many people whose command of English is non-existent or poor. At present, this includes those who have been granted indefinite leave to remain and who have been settled here for 3 years; refugees; asylum seekers receiving support; and persons with exceptional leave to remain and their spouses and children. In England, funding is provided through the Learning and Skills Council but different arrangements apply in Scotland and Wales where the respective Executives are responsible for basic skills provision. People who are here in categories leading to settlement also need to be encouraged to access courses as well as those already settled here and intending to seek British citizenship.

2.16   The Government intends to reconsider the eligibility criteria in order to ensure that discrepancies are remedied. In particular, spouses who are joining their partners here ought to be able to access these courses free of charge too. We will also try to ensure that any inconsistencies in provision in different parts of the country are ironed out.

2.17   A national core curriculum for ESOL, applicable in England, was published in December. The curriculum is context-free and we plan to develop learning programmes in a specific citizenship context so that a simple programme can be followed by those who need to develop an understanding in both language and citizenship. There will be consultation with interested bodies about the content of these new learning programmes. In the case of those who already have a good command of English, Welsh or Scottish Gaelic, suitable materials will be available to provide information about British society and the rights and responsibilities of becoming a British citizen.

2.18   We envisage these requirements extending to the spouses of applicants who are married to British citizens and British Dependent or Overseas Territories citizens who are not at present subject to the language requirement. The Government is concerned that everyone should be able to take a full and active part in British society. We do not think it is sufficient simply to rely on a spouse's knowledge of the language.

Celebrating the acquisition of citizenship

2.19   It is symptomatic of the low-key and bureaucratic approach which the UK has adopted to the acquisition of British citizenship that, unlike the position in many other countries, there are no arrangements for any kind of public act to mark becoming a British citizen. The use of citizenship ceremonies is well established in Australia, Canada and the United States and is becoming increasingly common in European countries. There is evidence to suggest that these ceremonies can have an important impact on promoting the value of naturalisation and that immigrant groups welcome them.[6]

2.20   The Government plans to address this by making provision in the forthcoming legislation for a citizenship ceremony to be held as an integral part of the naturalisation/registration process. This will give added significance to acquiring citizenship and provide an occasion at which individuals and their families and friends can mark the acquisition of citizenship. It also offers an opportunity for the State, and the local community, to welcome formally its new citizens.

2.21   The precise form of the citizenship ceremony will be subject to further consultation. But we envisage that ceremonies will be conducted by registration officers in Register Offices and other suitable places. These might include venues associated with community activity such as schools. They could be held either on a group or individual basis. Group ceremonies may reinforce the collective and community nature of citizenship. Whilst it would be inappropriate to ask those immediately entering the country to swear an oath, applicants for British citizenship currently swear an oath of allegiance to The Queen. We intend to modernise this oath so that it reflects a commitment to citizenship, cohesion and community. Specifically, in addition to allegiance to The Queen, it will make clear the fundamental tenets of British citizenship: that we respect human rights and freedoms, uphold democratic values, observe laws faithfully and fulfil our duties and obligations. It will be a citizenship pledge. This pledge will be at the heart of the new citizenship ceremony and will be the point at which citizenship will be conferred. A short statement of what it means to be a British citizen will also be issued

---

6   Simon Green, 'Citizenship for migrants', RDS (IRSS) commissioned research.

in the citizenship pack we are proposing to make available to all new applicants for British citizenship. It is not intended that existing citizens would have to take this new citizenship pledge. Our suggested, though not necessarily final, wording for the pledge is contained in Annex B. We would welcome any comments on it.

Updating our deprivation procedures

2.22   The Government believes that a corollary of attaching importance to British citizenship is that the UK should use the power to deprive someone of that citizenship – for example where it has been acquired through some form of deception or concealment and where that individual would not have been granted citizenship had they disclosed information requested from them. There is already a power to do this in the British Nationality Act 1981 although the last time someone was deprived of British citizenship was in 1973 using a similar power in the previous Act.

2.23   The Government intends to update the deprivation procedure and ensure that the arrangements contain appropriate safeguards. Action to deprive someone of British citizenship is always likely to be a rare event but the Government is willing to consider such action where it seems appropriate to do so. In particular, the Government will want to examine this option carefully in any case where someone has been granted British citizenship while concealing a material fact such as their past involvement in terrorism or war crimes. Although it is not always possible in such cases to take subsequent action to remove an individual from the UK, the Government considers that deprivation action would at least mark the UK's abhorrence of their crimes and make it clear that the UK is not prepared to welcome such people as its citizens (Chapter 7 provides further details of our proposals in respect of war criminals). This action would also enable us to withdraw protection provided to British citizens abroad and the representation which our extensive Diplomatic Service offers.

Reforming nationality legislation

2.24   The Government intends to introduce a number of provisions in the forthcoming legislation in order to update the British Nationality Act 1981 and to reflect modern thinking about citizenship. Among the more significant changes will be provisions:

   • Confirming, through repeal of the relevant provision, the Government's policy of giving reasons for refusal of nationality in all cases.

- Removing the present statutory distinctions between legitimate and illegitimate children where there is the required proof of paternity.
- Lowering from 10 years to 5 years the age at which certain children can be registered as British citizens under provisions for reducing statelessness.
- Removing the provision which currently limits the court's jurisdiction in reviewing nationality decisions.
- Removing the provisions in the amended Race Relations Act 1976 which permit discrimination where authorised by a Minister on the grounds of nationality, or ethnic or national origins, when carrying out nationality functions.

2.25   The Government is also considering how it might give effect to the suggestion made in paragraph 10.7 of the previous White Paper that in certain cases it might adopt a more flexible approach to the residence requirements in the 1981 Act. These require applicants for naturalisation to have been out of the UK for no more than 450 days during the 5 year qualifying period (270 days in the case of those with a 3 year qualifying period) and to have been absent for no more than 90 days in the year immediately preceding the date of application. Physical presence here is an important factor in measuring commitment to the UK and in facilitating integration. Accordingly, a substantial amount of residence ought normally to be expected of all applicants. The Act does, however, already allow flexibility over excess absences so the real issue to be resolved is how far this should extend and in what circumstances. We would welcome views on this question.

Chapter 3

WORKING IN THE UK

3.1   Full employment in the UK is one of the Government's overarching economic aims. Considerable progress has been made, with employment at record levels and unemployment at the lowest levels since the 1970s. However, there is still more to do. There remain 1.5 million unemployed including just under a million who are on benefits. In addition, there are 8 million who are not economically active – they are currently not looking for, or not able to take up, a job. These people include 4 million who are on 'inactive' benefits and whom the Government's Welfare to Work policies and Jobcentre Plus are helping to return to the labour market. Certain areas, groups and households are particularly disadvantaged in the labour market and suffer disproportionately from not having a job.

3.2   Our policies also need to ensure that, in addition to UK residents, people who come here from abroad play a full and productive part in the UK labour market and help to resolve the problems of recruitment difficulties and illegal working. These need to cover new entrants who have a permanent right to work in the UK (such as family settlers); those who are legally resident in the UK as refugees; and people from the rest of the EU who are legally able to work in the UK. This is in addition to people from outside the EU who enter the UK, initially on a temporary basis, through the work-related routes described in this Chapter.

3.3   Chapter 4 sets out the Government's integration strategy for refugees. Labour market policies for refugees are aimed at reducing the time it takes from entering the country to the point they are ready to move into work and hence reducing the pressure on recruitment difficulties and illegal working. So, our policies to speed up the asylum process and to integrate refugees more fully into UK society have the added economic advantage of increasing the productive potential of the economy. We are considering ways of extending integration measures to other groups of migrants. We are also working to reduce the barriers that may still exist which prevent EU citizens taking up vacancies in the UK. The European Commission has established a Skills and Mobility Task Force to help achieve this aim and we are co-operating fully with them.

3.4 Employers can face difficulties recruiting domestic labour for a variety of reasons. There may be a lack of suitably skilled, qualified or experienced applicants. There may be a time lag between training new or existing workers, or factors preventing the efficient matching of employers and workers. Employers may not be considering the full range of potential employees and workers may not have adequate information about job opportunities. Finally, domestic or EU workers may not be attracted to vacancies because of the pay or other conditions. Whatever the reason, in some cases, the jobs, and the goods and services they provide, would not exist without migrants to fill them.

3.5 The exact role for managed migration depends on the extent and nature of problems, bottlenecks and opportunities in the labour market. In the short run, migration may help to ease recruitment difficulties and skill shortages and also help to deal with illegal working. In the long run, if we are able to harness the vitality, energy and skills of migrants, we can stimulate economic growth and job creation. Identifying where skill shortages and recruitment difficulties are in the labour market, and what is causing them, is difficult. There is much anecdotal evidence but few sources that identify robustly the scale of labour needs and their skill levels. Annex C1 provides some details from the 2001 Employers Skills Survey (ESS)[7] that provides the most comprehensive picture of recruitment difficulties and skill shortages. Our assessment is that, although fewer than at equivalent points in past economic cycles, there are recruitment difficulties at both the high and low end of the skill spectrum and these have the potential to constrain productivity and the capacity for economic growth. These unfilled vacancies may also increase incentives and opportunities for illegal working, irregular migration and abuse of the asylum system.

3.6 This Chapter sets out the current routes of entry and proposals to augment and complement these routes to help satisfy our economic needs. This package of policies is not an alternative to developing the skills and productivity of, and employment opportunities for, the existing population. It is about providing a complement to these policies aimed at providing rational and credible legal routes for men and women who want to live and work in the UK, helping them to contribute to our economy. In addition, as part of a package of measures to tackle illegal working (outlined in Chapter 5), providing opportunities of work in the UK legally will reduce the need for economic migrants to enter and work clandestinely, often in vulnerable conditions, and for employers to recruit them to fill jobs. By allowing migrants to work legally

7 The Employers Skills Survey 2001 covers information from England. The Northern Ireland Skills Taskforce found a similar level of hard-to-fill vacancies attributable to skill shortages in a report published in October 2001. The Future Skills Wales Partnership and Scottish Enterprise will be carrying out similar surveys in 2003.

in the UK, this package will also transfer skills as well as money back to source countries. We will, (as outlined in Chapter 1), develop and adopt approaches to ensure that labour migration to the UK does not cause or exacerbate skills shortages in developing countries.

Current routes of entry

3.7   There are a range of different ways to enter the UK from outside the EU. Some of these entry routes are economic – the prime example is the work permit scheme. Others are primarily for visiting, studying or holiday-making, family reunion or humanitarian protection. Some routes are temporary; some may lead to settlement. This reflects our approach to managing migration which involves considering each of the migration routes – economic or not – and whether, and to what extent, they might play a part in achieving our objectives for the economy and the labour market.

Economic Routes

WORK PERMIT SCHEME

3.8   At present the main route of entry into the UK for economic purposes is the work permit scheme. The Executive Summary explained the major improvements in policy and procedure since a review in 2000. In 2001 there were over 104,000 new work permits issued (work permits and first permissions), in addition to around 33,000 extensions and changes of employment to existing permits. These figures, which include group workers, have increased from 80,000 new issues (work permits and first permissions) and 22,000 extensions and changes of employment in 2000. The work permit system is primarily designed to address recruitment of people outside the EU with medium and high skill levels, and to fill specific 'shortage occupations'.

3.9   The table below depicts work permit issues since 1946. From the early 1970s, work permits were no longer issued to unskilled and semi-skilled workers from outside the EU. Also, under the Immigration Act 1971, the issue of work permits was restricted to those coming to take up a specific job. Since the 1980s, the number of work permits has increased almost consistently, reflecting increasing international movement and 'brain circulation'.

Figure 2: Number of work permits and first permissions issued 1946-2000

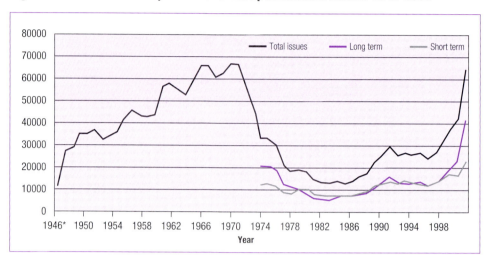

Source: Department of Employment (1977, 1981); Department for Education and Employment (unpublished); UK SOPEMI Reports (annual); Work Permits (UK).

3.10   An analysis of work permits and first permissions granted in 2000 by industry is presented in Home Office publication 'International migration in the UK: recent patterns and trends'[8] The figures show that 'computer services' and 'health and medical services' account for large proportions of the permits issued – 20% and 23% respectively. The high proportion of permits in these industries reflects the high growth of skill shortages in these areas. Work Permits (UK), now part of the Immigration and Nationality Directorate, will continue to work closely with employers, trades unions and sectoral advisory bodies to ensure we can continue to respond rapidly to changing labour market conditions. We will explore whether there is scope for further development or streamlining of the current arrangements, for example whether there would be benefits from easing the labour market test for highly skilled posts. In addition, we will continue to raise awareness of the service amongst small and medium size enterprises who need to recruit people from abroad to meet skill shortages.

Other routes to working in the UK

3.11   There are a range of other entry routes for people primarily wanting to work in the UK, including the Working Holidaymakers' Scheme, and routes for specific types of occupation. In addition, EU residents can enter the UK without any form of permit. Of the 760,000 non-visiting entrants to the UK in 2000, around 191,000 of them came here primarily to work[9].

8   Dobson, Koser, McLaughlan and Salt, 'International migration and the United Kingdom: Recent patterns and trends', RDS Occasional Paper 75, Home Office.

9   Salt et al, 'International migration in the UK: recent patterns and trends' forthcoming Home Office RDS Occasional Paper.

People from other EU countries accounted for around one quarter of all migrants living in the UK in 2000. Finally, opportunities exist under the General Agreement on Trade in Services (GATS) to move temporarily to the UK for the delivery of services.

3.12   The table below provides a summary of labour immigration to the UK for 2000. The categories listed are only those separately recorded for work related entry routes, and thus underestimate the total figure.

UK Labour Immigration 2000: Routes of Entry

	Number	Per cent
Work Permits (a)	67,100	35.1
Working Holidaymakers	38,500	20.1
EU (b)	35,700	18.7
Domestic Employees	14,300	7.5
Au Pairs	12,900	6.7
UK Ancestry	11,000	5.8
Seasonal Agricultural Workers	10,100	5.3
Ministers of Religion	1,180	0.6
Investors	50	0.0
Total	190,830	100.0

Source: Home Office admissions data, International Passenger Service (IPS),

(a) This describes the number of entrants to the UK with work permits and as such is a different figure to the number of work permits issued in 2000 (80,000).

(b) IPS.

3.13   People coming through other routes of entry (family reunion, for example, and those accepted as refugees) are also entitled to work, and contribute to the economic wealth of the country. The total of 190, 830 does not include the economically active family members and dependants of primary migrants, students or refugees. Overall, in 2000, foreign-born migrants made up 8% of the labour force.

New measures

3.14   We are enhancing our current routes of entry and tightening up our procedures through:

- The recent introduction of a Highly Skilled Migrant Programme to enable the most talented migrants to come to the UK.
- Charging for work permits.

- Making provisions in the Immigration Rules for certain postgraduate students to switch into employment.
- Considering ways to meet the demand for short-term casual labour.
- Reviewing the Working Holidaymaker scheme.
- Making sure that Ministers of Religion understand and appreciate the environment in which they will work and teach.
- Regulating those who provide advice and services in respect of work permits.

Highly Skilled Migrant Programme

3.15   The UK is competing for highly skilled workers with other countries keen to strengthen and enrich their economies by attracting highly skilled migrants. Countries are developing new and better ways of bringing in these workers.

3.16   The UK is a little ahead of the field in European terms, where much of the attention has focused on streamlining and speeding up work permit systems, a similar process to the work permit review already conducted and implemented in the UK. Other countries have eased access to their labour markets for dependants, increased the numbers of occupations which are exempt from labour market tests and made it easier for migrants to switch between employers and to switch from student status to work permit holder.

3.17   However some countries are making additional attempts to attract high skilled migrants. Germany is making a concerted effort to attract specific kinds of labour, in conjunction with development packages aimed at improving the skill base of its own population. Other countries, such as Australia and Canada, have well established 'points systems' allowing migrant workers who are sufficiently skilled to qualify to enter to find work. Some examples of recent measures taken by a selection of countries to attract highly skilled workers are included in Annex C2.

3.18   The UK allows the entry of some highly skilled migrants through our existing entrepreneurial routes, such as the Innovator Scheme and our employment-driven work permit system. We have now launched the Highly Skilled Migrant Programme. This represents a further step in developing our immigration system to maximise the benefits to the UK of high human capital individuals, who have the qualifications and skills required by UK businesses to compete in the global marketplace. The programme will allow highly skilled persons to migrate to the UK bringing with them new skills, talents and experiences. It will help eminent scientists to base their research projects here, and encourage the movement of business and financial experts to our centres of commerce. It will also facilitate the entry of doctors to work as general practitioners in the UK.

3.19   We have designed a flexible points-based system of assessment similar to that used in the Innovator Scheme. Individuals will be able to apply from overseas and will need to submit appropriate evidence of, amongst other things, educational qualifications, work experience, past earned income and their achievements in their chosen field. These conditions will ensure that successful applicants will make a significant contribution to the UK economy and society through employment, self-employment or engagement with business.

3.20   The programme will give those at the top of their chosen profession the choice of making the UK their home. Successful applicants will be granted leave to enter the UK initially for one year. We would expect these highly skilled people to find work quickly and, when they are employed at a level warranted by their skill base, they will be granted further leave to remain after this initial one year period. As with existing non-temporary routes, migrants entering under this scheme will be able to apply for settlement after they have been in the UK as Highly Skilled Migrants for four years. Likewise, principal applicants may seek entry for their spouse and dependent children. The programme will be marketed so that those in other countries are aware of its existence and the attraction of coming to the UK to look for work.

Charging for work permits

3.21   The work permit system already provides a fast, effective service. Service levels are exceptional with 90% of complete applications decided within one day of receipt. There is already a power to charge for after-entry immigration casework and plans are being made for charges to be introduced, linked to improvements in customer service. New powers to charge for work permits will also be introduced relieving pressure on general taxation.

Allowing students to switch into employment

3.22   Foreign students, whilst here to study, also have the potential to produce valuable benefits for the UK through joining the workforce at the end of their studies. Research clearly indicates that migrants with degree level qualifications can make significant economic contributions. Graduate migrant workers are likely to earn high wages, reflecting the valuable contribution they make to the UK economy and to the existing population through a positive fiscal contribution (i.e. they contribute more to Government revenue in taxes than they receive in benefits and public services)[10]. These contributions are enhanced by English language fluency and where qualifications are obtained in the UK[11].

3.23   In practice the Government already accepts applications from graduates who have finished their studies in the UK to enable them to switch into employment where they have a work permit. But we will make explicit provision in the Immigration Rules for graduating degree-level students, student nurses, and postgraduate doctors and dentists to transfer into the work permit employment category, where certain conditions are reached, including permission of any international sponsor. When considering individual applications for entry under this category, entry clearance officers at posts overseas will not refuse entry simply because the applicant wishes to consider working in the UK once they have completed their studies.

3.24   This policy will target those likely to make the greatest contribution to the United Kingdom and does not undermine other aspects of management of migration flows. To take advantage of this, students will need to obtain a work permit, have completed a degree at either a recognised UK further, or higher, education institution and have permission of any applicable international sponsor. Skilled, young people with close knowledge of United Kingdom economy and society will be able to stay in the UK to work where employment has been arranged. We will continue to market this policy change so that students who enter the UK to study are aware of the fact that they can stay here once they graduate.

Seasonal workers

3.25   There is a clear need for short-term casual labour. Although this comprises only a small proportion of all employment in the UK, it is important in industries such as agriculture. We will look again at the operation of the long-standing Seasonal Agricultural Workers' Scheme (SAWS) to see how it might better meet the needs of the agricultural sector. We will build on its principles to meet the demand for short-term casual labour in other sectors of the United Kingdom economy. As with the SAWS, we envisage quotas will be a key feature of any similar schemes that would be carefully targeted at specific sectors and closely managed. Entry would be for a short period of up to six months and applicants would not have the right to bring dependants with them.

10 Gott and Johnston, 'Migrants in the UK: fiscal effects', forthcoming Home Office RDS Occasional Paper.

11 Shields and Wheatley-Price, 'Migrants' labour market outcomes'. Forthcoming Home Office RDS Occasional Paper. For a summary see Glover et al. 'Migration: an economic and social analysis' RDS Occasional Paper No 67.

Working holidaymakers

3.26   There is a long-established Working Holidaymakers' Scheme. Under the scheme, young Commonwealth citizens come to the UK for an extended two-year holiday. Participants can take incidental employment to fund their stay here. Around 40,000 come to the UK each year on the scheme. Some Commonwealth countries have reciprocal schemes with the UK. The UK also has a bilateral youth exchange scheme with Japan.

3.27   Apart from the perceived cultural exchange benefits, the Commonwealth scheme provides an additional, temporary, flexible workforce. We are going to conduct a comprehensive review of the scheme in order to see whether we can build upon this element, considering it alongside our wider objectives for managing migration flows, to alleviate recruitment difficulties, contribute to sustainable economic growth, and reduce illegal working. We also want to ensure that the scheme is as inclusive as possible. At present, the majority of successful applicants come from Australia, New Zealand, Canada and South Africa.

3.28   We will work closely across Government to consider the different mechanisms and restrictions that can be applied to entrants, and how to achieve a balance between the Working Holidaymaker Scheme and the economic routes of entry to the UK. We will consider extending the principles behind the scheme and its operation to a wider range of countries, including to the EU candidate countries whose citizens will have a legal right to work in the UK in the years following accession. At the same time, we will look for ways to promote the existing scheme more successfully to all Commonwealth countries. We will also review the current restrictions on age and labour market activity, including what occupations people can work in, whilst still requiring participants to be self-sufficient. Removing such restrictions would enable people to undertake work at all skill levels. We will be consulting on these issues together with other matters, such as the size and length of this scheme and whether working holidaymakers should be able to switch into work permit employment. We will be issuing a consultation document in Spring 2002.

3.29   The development of these schemes will enable employers to recruit those with legal rights to work, undercutting the demand for labour currently supplied by illegal workers.

Ministers of religion

3.30   For many years, congregations with an employment vacancy that they cannot fill locally have been able to seek to appoint a Minister of religion from overseas. This applies to all religions recognised for the purposes of the Immigration Rules. Overseas ministers must be able to show, amongst other things, that they have been working as such or have been ordained. Between the years 1998-2000, the number of individuals entering the United Kingdom in this category has risen slightly, the figures being 1,040, 1,150 and 1,180 respectively.

3.31   Ministers of religion clearly have an important role to play in society. We are concerned that some of those who come to the UK for this purpose speak little or no English and therefore have little understanding of UK society. These difficulties may be compounded if they come from a rural background and are expected to work in an inner city area. This may make it hard for the individual to relate to the community in which they will teach and work and to play their part effectively as a religious leader, for example in discussions with the representatives of other faiths. This issue surfaced recently in the context of the reports into the disturbances last summer.

3.32   We therefore plan to allow appropriately qualified overseas persons already in the UK in another capacity, such as theological students, to switch their immigration status, in-country, to fill local vacancies as ministers. It is more likely that people who have already spent some time in the UK will be able to speak some English and have absorbed something of our culture and therefore be better able to relate their particular faith to the context of the United Kingdom. It will also be easier to verify the religious training or studies that the applicant will have been undertaking while in the UK. We have already begun consulting faith groups on this proposal.

3.33   To reinforce this, we will pursue the need for overseas applicants to demonstrate an appropriate command of English. Currently, entry clearance arrangements for those making applications overseas can be protracted. Information about the applicant's qualifications and background is difficult to obtain and we want to make sure that those granted entry in this capacity will be able to fulfil their role for the benefits of the community.

3.34   A guide to all the schemes referred to above are contained in Annex D.

Regulation of advice and services regarding work permit applications

3.35   As a significant legal entry route for work it is vital that those employers and individuals who use the Work Permit scheme can safely rely on those who advise and represent them in relation to work permit applications. The Government is committed to raising the standard of immigration advice and to control unscrupulous advisers through the regulatory scheme administered by the Office of the Immigration Services Commissioner (OISC) which was established under Part V of the Immigration and Asylum Act 1999. Work permit advice is often indivisible from immigration advice and there is a need for it to be brought unequivocally within the regulatory scheme. We therefore propose to amend Part V accordingly.

3.36   This will mean that the provision of work permit advice or services in the course of a business (paid or unpaid) will be prohibited unless a person is qualified within the meaning of Part V or exempted under the terms of the scheme. Anyone contravening the statutory provision will commit a criminal offence.

3.37   Details of the regulatory scheme are available from:

Office of the Immigration Services Commissioner
6th Floor
Fleetbank House
2-6 Salisbury Square
London EC4Y 8JX
Tel: 020 7211 1500
www.oisc.gov.uk

Chapter 4

ASYLUM

4.1 The disturbing sight of people risking life and limb to reach the UK from Sangatte through the Channel Tunnel illustrates graphically why we need to reform our asylum system. People are taking desperate measures to come to our country and we must develop a coherent policy which tackles the root cause of this desire and brings order to the system.

4.2 We will continue to honour our obligations not to return refugees who have arrived in the UK and to integrate fully those we recognise as refugees. But there is a world of difference between offering sanctuary to those in genuine fear of persecution and allowing asylum seekers to stay simply because the UK is their country of preference. The great majority of those seeking asylum could perfectly reasonably have sought protection at an earlier stage in their journey. Our clear message is if people want to come to the UK for economic reasons they must apply under the economic routes available to them as described in Chapter 3.

4.3 We must discourage this secondary movement by working internationally for a global system that delivers protection to those who need it. We need to recognise as well that not all those in need of protection will remain permanently in the country that helps them. As the international community intervenes in a particular country – like Afghanistan at present – with the consequential changes in government, the pressure for people to leave those countries can diminish, reversing the flow of people seeking protection elsewhere. What we do can influence the behaviour of others. We are playing a key role in discussions to establish sustainable solutions for global refugee issues. These include the UNHCR's Global Consultations on the operation of the 1951 Convention[12] and the European Commission's feasibility study of both extending protection to refugees in their region of origin and the establishment of a Europe-wide resettlement programme.

12 Under the 1951 Convention Relating to the Status of Refugees and its 1967 Protocol a refugee is defined as person who owing to a well-founded fear of being persecuted for reasons of race, religion, nationality, membership of a particular social group or political opinion, is outside the country of his nationality and is unable or, owing to such fear, is unwilling to avail himself of the protection of that country; or who, not having a nationality and being outside the country of his former habitual residence as a result of such events, is unable or, owing to such fear, is unwilling to return to it.

4.4 All EU countries face similar challenges in this area and we are working with European partners to address the issues on a much wider scale. In order to protect those in need and deal effectively with those who do not require protection, we need common asylum rules that are enforced in an equal and fair way across all EU countries. That is why, together with other EU Member States, we are committed to establishing sensible minimum standards for asylum procedures and policies as a basis for a common European asylum system where we will have EU-wide agreement on:

- A clear and workable definition of the State responsible for the examination of an asylum application.
- A fair and efficient asylum procedure.
- Minimum standards for reception conditions for asylum seekers.
- The approximation of rules on recognition and content of refugee status.

4.5 Applicants with well founded reasons for seeking asylum will be assured that their cases will be considered with care in the EU State responsible for entry. This will reduce the perceived pull factors of one country over another.

4.6 As part of this package of measures on asylum, the Dublin Convention[13] will be replaced with a mechanism reflecting the changed ways in which asylum seekers travel within Europe. It is important to uphold the principle of the Dublin Convention to avoid successive transfers of applicants without responsibility being taken to determine the asylum claim. And it is equally important to prevent parallel or successive claims and the related secondary movements known as 'asylum shopping'. A revised Dublin Convention mechanism will address more clearly the issue of Member State responsibility and act quickly to transfer asylum applicants to the state where responsibility lies. Other measures will guarantee proper procedures across the EU to ensure that asylum claims will be properly and efficiently dealt with wherever they are made. EU-wide minimum standards for living conditions for asylum seekers will ensure that one Member State is not perceived as a more attractive destination than another. All Member States will also give the same interpretation of refugee status so that differences in this area cannot be exploited by those seeking to take advantage of different systems.

4.7 However, waiting for final agreement on a pan-European basis does not resolve the immediate challenge that we face nor does it exempt us from taking all necessary steps to bring trust and confidence to the process both for asylum seekers and the broader community.

13 The Dublin Convention came into force on 1 September 1997. The basic principle underlying it is that asylum claims should be examined just once in the EU and that the Member State responsible for the presence of the asylum seeker in the EU should be responsible for concluding that examination.

Asylum applications in the UK

4.8   Like our European and other international partners we have seen an increase in the number of people coming to seek asylum on our shores. Figure 3 describes asylum applications between 1995 and 2001. Applications have been on a relatively steady upward trend over this period.

Figure 3: Asylum applications to the UK Quarter 1 1995 to Quarter 3 2001

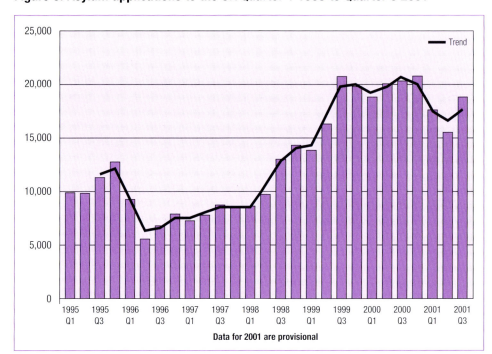

4.9   The number of asylum applications received in 2000 was 80,315, excluding dependants, 9,155 (13 per cent) more than in 1999[14]. But the increase in 2000 was the smallest percentage increase for three years (compared with year-on-year increases of 55 per cent in 1999 and 42 per cent in 1998). The main nationalities of applicants in 2000 were Iraqi (9 per cent), Sri Lankan (8 per cent), Federal Republic of Yugoslavia (FRY)[15] (8 per cent), Iranian (7 per cent) and Afghan (7 per cent).

14 Including dependents there were 98,900 applications in 2000 and 91,200 in 1999 (estimates rounded to nearest 100).

15 FRY is comprised of Kosovo, Serbia and Montenegro but the majority of FRY applications ate thought to be from Kosovars.

4.10   During 2001 the number of asylum applications has fallen – in January to September 2001 there were 52,155 applications, 12% lower than during the same period in 2000. The fall was largely due to lower numbers of applications from FRY, Chinese and Iranian nationals which were 53%, 55% and 29% lower respectively. At the same time, the numbers of applications from Afghanistan and Somalia rose by 74% and 37% respectively.

Asylum applications in the EU

4.11   Asylum applications, including dependants, to the 15 countries of the European Union, rose in 2000 for the fourth consecutive year, although this increase was just 1% compared with an increase of 27% in 1999 (from 396,700 in 1999 to 401,900 in 2000).

4.12   The UK ranked 9th amongst EU countries in terms of asylum seekers per head of population (with 1.7 asylum seekers per 1,000 national population)- slightly below 8th position in 1999. This compares with the largest international host countries, in this case Armenia, Guinea and FRY, who host 80, 59 and 46 refugees per 1,000 national population respectively[16]. The majority of asylum seekers, refugees, displaced persons and others of concern to the United Nations (UN) flee to neighbouring countries. UN estimates suggest that Iran currently hosts 1.9 million refugees and Pakistan hosts 2 million, for example.

Improvements to the asylum system

4.13   We have made significant progress in recent years. 132,000 decisions were made in the last financial year compared with 79,000 applications received. An estimated 43,000 asylum applications were awaiting an initial decision at 30 September 2001, just over a third of the level at its peak at the end of January 2000 (121,700).

4.14   Of the initial decisions made in 2000 under normal procedures, the Government granted refugee status to 10,375 applicants – 11 per cent of the total number of applications. Additionally, 11,495 applicants were granted exceptional leave to remain – 12 per cent of the total number of applications. But 75,680 applicants – 78 per cent – were refused asylum and did not qualify for exceptional leave. Of the 19,395 appeals determined in 2000, 3,340 -17 per cent – were allowed, 15,580 – 80 per cent – were dismissed, and the remainder were withdrawn or abandoned.

16 The statistics are from UNHCR and 2000 figures are provisional. UK figures are estimated by UNHCR on the basis of 10 years of refugee arrivals/asylum seeker recognition.

The key reforms

4.15   The Government is determined that the UK should have a humanitarian asylum process which honours our obligations to those genuinely fleeing persecution while deterring those who have no right to asylum from travelling here. That is why we are:

- Preparing a resettlement programme to establish gateways for those most in need of protection to come here legally.
- Introducing a managed system of induction, accommodation, reporting and removal centres to secure a seamless asylum process.
- Introducing an Application Registration Card to provide more secure and certain evidence of identity and nationality.
- Phasing out voucher support.
- Better assisting Unaccompanied Asylum Seeking Children and sharing support for these children across a wider number of local authorities while sifting out adults posing as children.
- Streamlining our appeals system to minimise delay and cut down barriers to removal.
- Increasing the number of removals of people who have no claim to stay here.
- Enhancing refugee integration through our Refugee Integration Programme and labour market measures.

Resettlement programme

4.16   The Government accepts that it is often very difficult for those who do have a well-founded fear of persecution to arrive in the UK legally to seek our help. The absence of such provision provides succour to the traffickers and exposes the most vulnerable people to unacceptable risks. We propose to develop ways in which refugees, whose lives cannot be protected in their region of origin, can have their claim considered before they reach the UK and are able to travel here in safety and receive protection. A UK resettlement programme would sit at the heart of these gateways. Resettlement is a sustainable and long-term solution to the problems faced by refugees and has worked successfully in other countries.

4.17   The UK's resettlement programme would operate in addition to current asylum determination procedures, and would build on our partnerships with international and domestic refugee bodies, including the UNHCR, the Red Cross, and the International Organisation for Migration (IOM).

4.18   In developing the detail of the programme's operation, we will look into its possible size, practical operation, and how best it may provide long term protection to those most in need. One possibility is for the UK to set a quota each year working closely with the UNHCR to identify resettlement needs. We would set eligibility criteria to be used by UNHCR field officers in identifying suitable candidates. We might then conduct missions to interview the candidates and to discuss the case with the field officers. We would then make a decision on the candidate's suitability, probably after a referral to our offices in the UK where security and other screening checks could be carried out.

4.19   We will take into account the work currently being done by the European Commission to establish the feasibility of a Europe-wide programme, as well as the excellent examples set by those of our European neighbours who operate similar schemes: Denmark, Finland, the Netherlands, and Sweden; and our colleagues further afield: Australia, Canada, New Zealand and the United States. This will lead to the development of detailed proposals on which we will consult fully with interested parties. A guide to how the scheme could work is at Annex E.

Induction Centres

4.20   Induction centres are the first stage in achieving a holistic approach to the handling of asylum seekers' applications – from arrival to the removal of failed applicants, or the integration into the community of those recognized as refugees.

4.21   Induction Centres provide the opportunity for a comprehensive service to asylum seekers so that they are fully aware of how our procedures work and understand exactly what is expected of them. The Government intends to provide briefing explaining in detail the processes involved, including information about the area to which the asylum seeker will be dispersed and how to make a voluntary departure should they no longer wish to pursue an asylum claim. The briefing will be carried out both orally by staff and by video in the principal languages used by asylum seekers. We will also supply additional briefing literature including information about access to legal advice. Before leaving the induction centre, there will be a requirement for all asylum seekers to sign a document confirming that they understand:

- The processes that accompany their claim for asylum and support.
- Their obligations to comply with temporary admission and reporting arrangements.
- The requirement to leave the UK should their asylum claim fail.
- How they can obtain assistance to return.

4.22 Making sure asylum seekers understand what will happen to them is an essential part of our reforms. But the induction process is about more than explanations. Basic health screening will be available assisting in the early identification of special needs. An asylum interview will be booked and a letter of invitation to the interview, together with a travel warrant, will be handed to the asylum seeker.

4.23 Asylum seekers will remain in the induction centres for a short period of time, approximately 1-7 days:

- Those who do not require support will remain for I day after which they will move to an agreed address under the terms of their temporary admission.
- Those who will be accommodated at an Accommodation Centre will remain for around 2 days whilst travel arrangements are made.
- Those seeking support from the National Asylum Support Service (NASS) will remain for approximately 7 days during which time their application for support will be decided, taking into account personal means. Arrangements will be made for dispersal to accommodation throughout the UK.

4.24 The Induction Centre buildings will house between 200-400 asylum seekers and their dependants, providing full-board accommodation. There will be smaller units of accommodation for single or pregnant women or special needs cases. The Induction Centres will be located close to, or within easy travelling distance of, major asylum intake areas with a small number in regional areas. This will help reduce the pressure on bed and breakfast accommodation.

Application Registration Cards

4.25 On departure from the Induction Centres, we will give asylum seekers an Application Registration Card (ARC). These will replace the Standard Acknowledgement Letters (SALs) which are currently used for identification of asylum seekers and which are widely susceptible to fraud and counterfeiting. The ARCs will be biometric smart cards containing personal details including a photograph, fingerprints and employment status. They will contain modern physical security features giving much better protection against forgery and counterfeiting and allowing fast verification of identity. We will not replace lost ARCs unless a fingerprint check has been conducted.

4.26   The ARC will be used in a number of situations:

- It will become a routine part of the reporting procedure and will contain details specifying the next date on which the holder must report.
- Those claiming NASS support will be expected to present an ARC at the Post Office at the time of payment.
- They will be a much more reliable form of identification for use in everyday transactions such as registering with a doctor.
- They will assist immigration officers to establish identity during enforcement operations.

4.27   The Government will carry out an audit of all known SAL holders and will replace their SAL with an ARC. On completion, the SAL will no longer be a valid document. We will require all asylum seekers claiming support to obtain and present an ARC. We have already begun to issue the first ARCs.

Accommodation Centres

4.28   The Government is committed to ensuring that asylum seekers are properly supported and accommodated whilst their claims are being considered. This entails both rights and responsibilities for asylum seekers, who will be expected to keep in touch with the relevant authorities and to provide all the necessary information for their claims to be considered. In return, asylum seekers can expect to be offered support and accommodation, where it is needed, and to be offered assistance with integration or return.

4.29   It is in the interests of all parties – the applicant, the local community and central and local government – that asylum applications are considered quickly and efficiently. For this reason, the Government has considered options for supporting asylum seekers which also contribute to the efficient management of the asylum system.

4.30   The Government will establish a number of new Accommodation Centres, with a total capacity of approximately 3,000, to accommodate a proportion of new asylum seekers from application through initial decision and any appeal. This will be taken forward on a trial basis.

4.31   The centres will provide full-board accommodation. Services, including health care, education, interpretation and opportunities for purposeful activities will also be provided for. The latter may include activities such as training in English language and IT skills, and volunteering in the local community.

4.32   In the course of the trial we want to assess whether the provision of a broad range of facilities within the Accommodation Centres provides a more supportive environment for asylum seekers than is often available under the current dispersal arrangements. At the same time, we will examine the effect of the Centres in reducing delays in the processing of cases and whether they facilitate more efficient decision-making. Accommodation Centres are a new concept in the UK, but are widely used across Europe.

4.33   A proportion of new asylum seekers who are eligible for NASS support will be allocated places in Accommodation Centres. Those who request support and who are eligible for it and meet the Accommodation Centre criteria, will be expected to accept the offer of a place. Those who refuse such an offer will not be offered any alternative forms of support. Once the new arrangements are up and running, the option of receiving voucher-only or cash-only support will no longer be available.

4.34   For the trial period, immigration staff will apply a number of criteria when determining the allocation of these places. These will include the following:

- A suitable place. The trial centre will need to be able to cater for living and support needs.
- Language. We intend that the number of core languages spoken in each centre should be limited. This will help to ensure that relevant interpreters can be provided and will assist in the development of viable communities within each centre. This is consistent with one of the findings of the dispersal review[17] which proposed a return to clustering on the basis of language wherever possible.
- Family circumstances. Clearly we do not yet know what the detailed make-up of each site will be but, whether the asylum seeker is single, has a partner and/or has dependent children will be important factors in the allocation process to ensure that appropriate accommodation and services are available.
- The port of entry or Induction Centre. During the trial, the limited number of places may necessitate additional selection criteria. As far as possible, this will be done in an open and objective way. Particularly in the early days of the trial, the allocation of places may be limited to those arriving at certain ports, or those passing through certain Induction Centres. This will also enable direct links to be established between a particular port or Induction Centre and the nearest Accommodation Centre.

4.35   During the trial, allocation decisions will be taken on an individual basis based on clear criteria. But, even where individuals meet the normal criteria for allocation to a trial centre, immigration staff will have the discretion to make exemptions to reflect exceptional

17 Report of the operational reviews of the voucher and dispersal schemes of the National Asylum Support Service, Home Office, October 2001.

circumstances. This might include cases where the asylum seeker has special needs which could not be catered for in an Accommodation Centre or where, for particular reasons, they might be considered a risk if allocated to such a centre.

4.36   Asylum seekers will not be detained in Accommodation Centres. They will be able to come and go, and will receive a small cash allowance for incidental expenses. They will also be entitled to receive visitors. Accommodation Centre residents will have access to legal advice either on site or by co-ordinated local advice services. Legal advisors may or may not be based on site, depending on the particular circumstances at each centre. Where advisors are not to be based permanently on site, facilities will be provided for consultations with visiting advisors. Arrangements at each centre will be decided and funded by the Legal Services Commission. While access to legal advice is not a pre-requisite to initial decision making, and should not hold up the decision making process, the Government is committed to ensuring access to quality legal advice at that, and all later stages, for all asylum seekers whether or not they are in an Accommodation Centre.

4.37   Residents will be subject to a residence requirement. This means that they will be required to reside at the allotted centre throughout the processing of their application and will be required to report regularly to confirm that they are complying with this requirement.

4.38   Residents of Accommodation Centres who breach these requirements will be left in no doubt that their actions may affect the outcome of their asylum claim, where the non-compliance damages their credibility.

4.39   In evaluating the trial of Accommodation Centres, the Government will assess whether the centres facilitate improvements in the asylum process, including, for example:

- Closer contact between asylum seekers and the relevant authorities.
- Reduced decision times by tighter management of the interview and decision-making process.
- Fewer opportunities for illegal working during the application process.
- Minimal opportunities for financial or housing fraud.
- Reduction in community tensions.
- Facilitation of integration for those granted a status in the UK and voluntary return. packages for those who are refused (see paragraphs 4.85-4.89 for more information on voluntary returns).

4.40   The Government is committed to ensuring that the long-term mix of facilities for the support of asylum seekers and management of the asylum processes is based on evidence of what works. The operation of the trial Accommodation Centres will be thoroughly evaluated, taking account of a number of factors, including costs, processing times, ease of access to integration programmes for those granted refugee status and the rate of returns in cases which are refused.

4.41   Accommodation Centres will only serve a proportion of asylum seekers. Apart from those selected for fast-track processing at Oakington Reception Centre (see paragraphs 4.69-4.72) or otherwise detained, the remainder of asylum seekers in need of support will be placed in dispersal accommodation. The Government will maintain the principle of dispersal away from London and the South East but develop better mechanism for consultation with, and the involvement of, local authorities and others. Taking account of the practical and financial impact on local services, we will revert to a policy of dispersal based on language cluster areas.

Reporting

4.42   Maintaining contact with asylum seekers is essential. Those in Accommodation Centres may be required to report on a daily basis within the Accommodation Centre. Those dispersed and those who do not require NASS accommodation will also be required to report at the NASS address, at reporting centres or at police stations attended by staff from the Immigration and Nationality Directorate. During the induction process asylum seekers will be advised of their obligations to notify any change of address and to report as required. Provision of support will be made conditional on asylum seekers reporting as required.

4.43   The reporting process will produce confirmation of the applicant's current address thereby validating other records. Asylum seekers failing to report as required will be liable to have their support terminated. The ARC will play a fundamental part in the reporting and validation process (see paragraphs 4.25-4.27).

4.44   The introduction of Accommodation Centres and increased use of reporting will be accompanied by new arrangements for some initial decisions and appeal determinations to be served by staff of the Immigration and Nationality Directorate to ensure that the asylum seeker receives the relevant paperwork. The asylum seeker will have 10 days in which to submit an appeal against the decision and may be required to report during and at the end of this period. Appeals determinations may be served in reporting centres, at police stations, at Accommodation Centres and at home addresses.

4.45   The Government recognises there are practical difficulties in requiring people to report to reporting centres some distance from their accommodation. We currently require anyone who is within 90 minutes by public transport or 25 miles radius of a reporting centre to report to that reporting centre. This can be costly to the asylum seeker. We are reviewing the policy to identify suitable alternatives which would ease the financial pressure for asylum seekers. A mobile reporting team is being trialled at Leicester. The plan is to increase the number of mobile reporting teams to cover key police stations not served by static reporting centres or National Asylum Support Service teams.

4.46   These new practices will introduce more rigorous control into the asylum process and will lead to improved contact with asylum seekers. The aim is to achieve stronger management of the asylum process, whilst also affording asylum seekers further opportunities to monitor their cases.

REGIONALISATION

4.47   The National Asylum Support Service (NASS) is currently organised on a highly centralised and functional basis but the service is delivered regionally. In line with the recommendations of last autumn's review of the dispersal system, NASS is re-orientating its business activities to reflect better the needs across the country and to improve business delivery. It is currently developing the processes, mechanisms and structures to achieve this.

4.48   The aim is to deliver a service that is better managed, more empowered and better resourced. Not only will this mean that more resources will be deployed regionally but also that those resources that are already there will be better used. The outcome will be a more joined-up NASS and one that has a better fit with the environment in which it works. The dispersal review recommended that the relevant Regulations should be amended to change the notice period for ending asylum support from 14 days to 21 days for failed asylum seekers and to 28 days for those granted leave to remain. We are making arrangements to implement this change. Furthermore, there is a case for much more effective use and reallocation of existing resources to aid integration for those granted asylum. We will be examining this in the weeks ahead.

INTERPRETATION

4.49   In September 2000 we established the Central Interpreters Unit to provide a consistent, professional approach to interpreters across the Immigration and Nationality Directorate. Applicants can be British or EU citizens or those with indefinite leave to remain here. 2000 interpreters have now received the required training at many ports and casework offices across the UK including the dispersal areas.

Audit of existing asylum seekers

4.50   The new arrangements for tighter contact management of asylum seekers must also be applied to existing applicants. Some are already subject to reporting requirements. Many others are still being supported from public funds, either by the National Asylum Support Service (NASS) or local authorities, but have not been required to report regularly for their status to be monitored.

4.51   The Government is already working with local authorities to agree the details of all asylum seekers at present receiving local authority support. That information, together with details of those receiving direct NASS support or who are subject to potential removal even though not supported, will be used to conduct an audit of all existing asylum seekers. In each case, the current status of the application will be checked. Unless it is clear that the case can be resolved, either by granting some status in the light of changed circumstances or by immediate removal action, the applicant will be required to report to the Immigration and Nationality Directorate. Their fingerprints will be taken and an Application Registration Card (ARC) will be issued if appropriate. The applicant will also be interviewed to establish any significant change in circumstances and a requirement for further regular reporting will be imposed as necessary. Those who fail to report when required to do so will be liable to have any support they may be receiving withdrawn. In this way, the audit and the new processes, including issue of ARCs to all new applicants, will reduce fraud and multiple applications and enable robust contact management of all asylum seekers throughout the process. This is a vital part of our determination to get to grips with long-standing cases.

Phasing out voucher support

4.52   The Government intends to phase out the voucher system during the latter part of 2002. Asylum seekers placed in Accommodation Centres will have no need for voucher support. We are pursuing mechanisms to provide financial support for asylum seekers and cash will replace vouchers. The outcome will be a robust scheme less prone to fraud and which avoids the stigma felt by many asylum seekers under the voucher scheme. In the meantime we are committed to increasing the total value of voucher support in line with the most recent income support rises. The value of vouchers will increase by around 1.6%. The value of the voucher which is exchangeable for cash will rise from £10 to £14.

4.53   Some asylum seekers are able to support themselves without requiring NASS support or an Accommodation Centre place. Others have vouchers but no accommodation from NASS. For the future, the case for abolishing the 'voucher only' option will be looked at and a power to allow this will be taken in forthcoming legislation.

Unaccompanied Asylum Seeking Children

4.54   We will continue to offer protection and appropriate levels of care to children under the age of 18 who have been separated from their parents and other family and who are genuinely in need of protection. In pursuing this objective the Home Office will continue to work closely with the Department of Health and local authorities, as well as with Non-Governmental Organisations (NGOs) and interested children's groups. The Home Office leads the Unaccompanied Asylum Seeking Children's Stakeholder Group containing representatives from local authorities, NGOs, voluntary organisations and the Department of Health. This group meets quarterly and is the main forum for taking forward issues requiring wide consultation and joint working.

4.55   To do this effectively we need to identify children in genuine need at the earliest possible stage, to sift out adults posing as children and to deter those seeking to abuse the system.

4.56   Home Office staff are already taking steps to challenge older applicants and to divert them to the adult asylum process so that adults posing as children do not become a problem for local authorities. And specialist teams of caseworkers in the Immigration and Nationality Directorate aim to make initial decisions on at least 60% of new applications from unaccompanied children within 2 months.

4.57   We have also tightened up our exceptional leave policy in respect of unaccompanied children so that those who do not qualify for asylum or protection but for whom care in their own country cannot be arranged are given leave in the UK only until their 18th birthday.

4.58   We will also be amending the Immigration Rules to enable immigration staff to interview children about their claims in a wider set of circumstances than is the case now. We believe that many children would welcome the opportunity to tell their story, and a better understanding of a child's background and experiences will enhance the ability of the Home Office and local authorities to offer appropriate levels of protection and care in each case. Home Office staff are being trained for this purpose, and no-one will be allowed to interview children about their claim unless they have received the necessary training.

4.59   Local authorities must also be able to meet their care responsibilities. The vast majority of asylum seeking children are supported by local authorities in London and the South East and some find it difficult to provide the levels of care to which they are committed.

4.60   We will do more to support local authorities by improving information exchange, communications and models of best practice in the care of unaccompanied minors, including preparations for return or for leaving care. We will explore opportunities for joint commissioning of suitable accommodation for unaccompanied minors who are 16 or 17 on arrival, subject to an assessment of individual needs, perhaps located away from the South East but with robust arrangements for social care under the Children Act. It is important that financial support to local authorities provides fairly for essential needs and encourages good value for money.

Asylum appeals

4.61   The effect of improved induction, accommodation and reporting will be limited if we do not address delays within the appeals system. The Immigration and Asylum Act 1999 introduced a one-stop appeal system requiring an adjudicator considering an asylum appeal also to deal with any other appealable matters raised by the applicant. The principle has worked well but the provisions of the Act have not always been as easy to understand. The introduction of human rights appeals also meant that some of those who had exhausted all other appeal rights before the coming into force of the Act in October 2000 used them simply as a means to delay removal. This has led to the appeal system becoming clogged up and unable to deal effectively with the new appeals in a timely way.

4.62   The Government proposes to re-structure the legislation to simplify the one-stop appeal provisions. We will remove the unnecessary repetition of processes, lack of clarity, inconsistencies and omissions. We will make it clear that there will be a single right of appeal, triggered by the service of listed decisions, subject to exceptions on listed grounds. We want to ensure that human rights claims are dealt with in a timely fashion and do not frustrate the removals process.

4.63   We will:

- Define the specific immigration decisions which attract a right of appeal.
- Make clear that Removal Directions which are an administrative decision flowing from an earlier refusal decision which is itself appealable, will not be one of the immigration decisions which attract a right of appeal.

- Take steps to ensure that we can certify cases where a failed asylum seeker has been given an opportunity to appeal but has chosen not to do so.
- Take a power to set a date by which human rights claims must be submitted. Thereafter any such claim will not attract a right of appeal if it is refused.

4.64   Our proposals to track asylum seekers through the system will ensure that, for those who do not appeal or whose appeal has failed, we overcome the recurrent problem of not being able to locate a failed asylum seeker. We intend also to introduce personal delivery of some asylum appeal determinations, concentrating initially on unsuccessful appeal cases where statutory rights of appeal have been exhausted. Previously, the appellant has been notified at the same time as the Home Office allowing a high level of absconding on receipt of the determination. This is purely a method of communicating the decision and does not affect its independence or any rights of appeal. We will evaluate this method and consider expanding it to include all reporting centres and all appeal determinations.

4.65   We will simplify the current appeals system by ending the procedure for certification of certain cases by the Secretary of State which permits a right of appeal to an adjudicator only, provided that the adjudicator agrees that the certificate was properly made. This will increase access to the Immigration Appeal Tribunal.

4.66   We intend to make sure that appeals progress through the system without unnecessary delays. The Home Office and Lord Chancellor's Department are working closely on ways to accomplish this:

- There are far too many appeals which are adjourned and in many cases we believe that requests are made which are little more than a tactic to delay the outcome and therefore the removal of failed asylum seekers. A statutory closure date to prevent multiple adjournments of a case at the adjudicator stage will be introduced.
- We will require all appeals to be made in a prescribed way and time with a presumption that the more out of time an appeal is, without good reason, the greater the onus will be on the adjudicator not to allow it to proceed.

We also want to see further streamlining through:

- A more structured use of 'fast-tracking' applied to appeals to the Tribunal.
- Making the Immigration Appeal Tribunal a Superior Court of Record. This will reflect the fact that a high court judge heads the Tribunal and recognises the importance of its jurisdiction. As a Superior Court of Record there should be no scope for judicial review of its decisions, particularly of refusals to grant leave to appeal that are made in an attempt

to frustrate removal. The Tribunal will focus entirely on the lawfulness of adjudicators' decisions rather than their factual basis. There will also still be a right of appeal from the Tribunal to the Court of Appeal on a point of law.

JUDICIAL REVIEW

4.67   Judicial review is not an appeal as such but the means by which an individual can challenge the decision of any public authority on the grounds of legality and/or fairness. In the interests of discouraging those who pursue unmeritorious cases and of promoting a proper use of public money we want to ensure that the merits test for controlled legal representation funded by the Legal Services Commission is applied properly by representatives. We also want to seek ways to reduce the time taken for the judicial review process in cases where removal directions have been set. These are all measures to tighten up existing procedures which will not reduce access to judicial review for deserving applicants.

INCREASING JUDICIAL CAPACITY AND THE AVAILABILITY OF GOOD QUALITY LEGAL ADVICE

4.68   The Government will increase capacity by 50 per cent. The number of cases with hearings before an adjudicator will increase from the current 4,000 to 6,000 cases a month by November this year. We are expanding all the key elements in the process. Since early 2000, the number of courtrooms has risen from 35 to 103; adjudicator appointments from 285 to 399; and interpreters have more than doubled from 600 to 1300. We are also expanding the number of good quality legal advisers available as the number of solicitors' firms and not-for-profit agencies with quality assured immigration contracts with the Legal Services Commission has increased to 581 as at December last year. Similar increases will occur to manage the additional 2000 cases a month.

Oakington Reception Centre

4.69   The Oakington Reception Centre facility is a key element within the Government's overall strategy for processing asylum applications as speedily as possible. It is a central plank of asylum policy and is coupled with a fast track appeals process which brings those applications determined as unfounded quickly to the point of being returnable whilst helping to minimise support costs.

4.70   The facility enables certain asylum applications to be decided quickly, within about 7-10 days. In order to achieve that objective for significant numbers of applicants, an intensive consideration and decision process is required, making full use of each of the 7-10 days to keep to an absolute minimum the duration of stay. It is necessary for applicants to be available for an early interview and to submit any further representations that may be judged necessary. It is also important that they should be readily available for the decision to be served. The Government's experience is that many applicants, particularly those whose applications are likely to be unfounded, are unwilling to comply with the fast track procedures. In the Government's view, the Oakington regime and its use of statutory detention powers, is necessary and appropriate in order to achieve the objective of speedy decision making of a substantial number of claims.

4.71   Oakington is designated as a place of detention and applicants referred there are detained. Although the facilities provided are in keeping with those in immigration removal centres, the practical operation is different. In particular, there is a relaxed regime with minimal physical security, reflecting the fact that the purpose is to consider and decide applications speedily. To facilitate the fast track decision process, and subsequent fast track appeals for unfounded applicants, there is free and independent legal advice available on site, provided by the Refugee Legal Centre and Immigration Advisory Service. The Refugee Council also has staff based at Oakington who assist the National Asylum Support Service in determining applicants' eligibility for Government support should they be released at the end of the process.

4.72   At full capacity, it is possible for about 250 applicants to be processed each week, up to a maximum of 13,000 in a full year. Deciding this volume of asylum applications in about 7-10 days represents a major contribution to Government targets and enables asylum applicants and their families to know quickly whether they have any basis to remain in the United Kingdom.

Removals

4.73   In June 2001, the Home Secretary set out a target of removing 2,500 failed asylum seekers a month leading to the removal of 30,000 by Spring 2003. To maximise our capabilities we have:

- Launched a joint protocol with the police. The protocol establishes a mechanism whereby the police will assist and support the Immigration Service in the removal of immigration offenders. It also aims to develop Immigration Service expertise in the arrest of immigration offenders without the support of the police whilst ensuring the safety of immigration officers. The aims must be achieved in a way that maintains and increases the trust and confidence of the public, and particularly members of ethnic communities.
- Used charter flights to remove large numbers of failed asylum seekers. Since March 2001, 1,707 Kosovan Albanians have been removed in this way. Despite the cost of charter flights, this is a very efficient way of enforcing the volume departure of those who have no right to stay here.

- Increased resources to handle the difficulties of removing people who do not have a travel document. The Immigration Service has to apply to Foreign Embassies and High Commissions for travel documents to assist in increasing the number of removals of undocumented passengers who may have disposed of or lost their original papers. In 2000, we processed 1,570 travel document applications increasing to 2,660 by April 2001. We are allocating additional staff to deal with the expected increase in applications.

We will also:

- Establish the National Intelligence Model across the Immigration and Nationality Directorate so that intelligence will be sought from and shared with other systems within IND and outside. The success of this approach has already been shown where IND has a key role within the National Criminal Intelligence Service in combating organised and transnational crime (see Chapter 5 for more information).
- Set up a confidential Immigration Hotline to enable members of the public to report immigration abuse.

REMOVAL CENTRES

4.74   Detention has a key role to play in the removal of failed asylum seekers and other immigration offenders. To reinforce this we shall be redesignating existing detention centres, other than Oakington Reception Centre, as 'Removal Centres'. Detention remains an unfortunate but essential element in the effective enforcement of immigration control. The primary focus of detention will continue to be its use in support of our removals strategy.

4.75   We have expanded the number of immigration detention places from about 900 in 1997 to just under 2,800 by the end of 2001. The new Removal Centres at Harmondsworth, Yarl's Wood and Dungavel which opened during 2001 accounted for 1,500 of these additional places. We have decided to increase detention capacity by a further 40%, to 4,000 places, in order to facilitate an increased rate of removals of failed asylum seekers and others with no basis of stay in the UK. Work to identify suitable sites is underway and we expect to have all the additional places in operation by Spring 2003.

DETENTION CRITERIA

4.76   Although the main focus of detention will be on removals, there will continue to be a need to detain some people at other stages of the process. Our 1998 White Paper set out the criteria by which Immigration Act powers of detention were exercised and confirmed that the starting point in all cases was a presumption in favour of granting temporary admission or release. The criteria were modified in March 2000 to include detention at Oakington Reception

Centre if it appeared that a claimant's asylum application could be decided quickly. The modified criteria and the general presumption remain in place. There has, however, been one change in terms of the detention criteria as they relate to families.

4.77 Families can in some instances give rise to the same problems of non-compliance and thus the need to detain as can be encountered with single adults. Naturally there are particular concerns about detaining families and it is not a step to be taken lightly. Although true of all decisions to detain, it is especially important in the case of families that detention should be used only when necessary and should not be for an excessive period. It was previously the case that families would, other than as part of the fast-track process at Oakington Reception Centre, normally be detained only in order to effect removal. Such detention would be planned to take place as close to removal as possible so as to ensure that families were not normally detained for more than a few days. Whilst this covered most circumstances where detention of a family might be necessary, it did not allow for those occasions when it is justifiable to detain families at other times or for longer than just a few days. Accordingly, families may, where necessary, now be detained at other times and for longer periods than just immediately prior to removal. This could be whilst their identities and basis of claim are established, or because there is a reasonable belief that they would abscond. Where families are detained they are held in dedicated family accommodation based on family rooms in Removal Centres. No family is detained simply because suitable accommodation is available.

PRISON SERVICE ACCOMMODATION

4.78 The use of Prison Service accommodation to hold immigration detainees has been a matter of understandable concern and we have pursued a strategy to eliminate our reliance on this accommodation, subject to limited exceptions. Part of this strategy has centred on the opening of new Immigration Service Detention Centres. This has allowed us to withdraw from the small number of local prisons across the country which were used as a temporary measure to provide much needed detention places. This withdrawal was completed in mid-January. We have also ceased to use the dedicated accommodation in part of HMP Rochester. In addition, the dedicated immigration detention facilities at HMP Haslar and HMP Lindholme will shortly be redesignated formally as Removal Centres: this will require them to operate under the Detention Centre Rules and, together with other administrative changes, will bring them fully into line with other Removal Centres. Haslar and Lindholme will be joined by HMYOI Dover in the Spring when that establishment too is redesignated as a Removal Centre.

4.79   It will always remain necessary to hold small numbers of immigration detainees, including asylum seekers, in prison for reasons of security. This would include suspected international terrorists detained under the Anti-terrorism, Crime and Security Act 2001. Any asylum seeker who is held on suspicion of having committed a criminal offence or is serving a custodial sentence will also be held in prison.

SERIOUS CRIMINALS

4.80   We will explore what more we can do, as other countries have done, to stop serious criminals abusing our asylum system by seeking to remain in the UK having completed a custodial sentence.

STRENGTHENING POWERS

4.81   We propose to extend the existing power of detainee escorts to search detained persons to allow their entry to private premises to conduct such searches. Searching people being taken into detention is necessary to ensure the safety and security of the detainees themselves as well as of those escorting them. Detainee escorts do not presently have an express right to enter private premises to search a detained person. In the case of a person being taken into detention from their home or other private premises the absence of this right of entry usually means that the person concerned has to be taken to a nearby police station before they can be searched by the escort. This causes unnecessary delay, unwanted burdens on the police and, potentially, needless distress to the detained persons. We propose to solve this problem by providing detainee escorts with a statutory right to enter private premises in order to search detained persons. This limited right would be exercisable only as part of an escort arrangement and only whilst accompanying a police or immigration officer.

4.82   We are continuing to look at ways of reducing delays to the process of removal. We want to eliminate procedural delays arising from the need to pass files between different parts of the organisation. We will use the forthcoming legislation to restore the former power allowing staff outside the Immigration Service to detain overstayers or to require them to report at regular intervals. They will also have a corresponding power in respect of illegal entrants. This will complement powers already available to set reporting conditions for certain categories of arriving passenger and the power to detain or release on conditions a person facing deportation.

BAIL

4.83   Part III of the Immigration and Asylum Act 1999 created a complex system of automatic bail hearings at specified points in a person's detention. It has never been brought into force. As part of our revision of immigration and asylum processes we propose to repeal most of Part

III. We will implement section 53, which allows for regulations to be made in respect of the existing arrangements for seeking bail, and section 54, which removes an anomaly from those arrangements that prevented certain people from applying for bail. The remainder of Part III is now inconsistent with the need to ensure that we can streamline the removals process in particular and immigration and asylum processes more generally. The significant and continuing expansion of the detention estate since the proposals were first put forward would make the system unworkable in practice. But the existing bail arrangements, which enable detainees to apply to an adjudicator or chief immigration officer for bail, will remain in place and will continue to ensure that asylum seekers and others who are detained have effective opportunities to seek and, where appropriate, be granted bail.

4.84   We propose to make one change to those existing arrangements. At present, other than where applications are made to Adjudicators, bail can be granted only by an immigration officer not below the rank of chief immigration officer. As part of ongoing organisational changes within IND and, in particular, the need to ensure that Immigration Service staff are deployed to best effect, bail applications will in future no longer be dealt with exclusively by Immigration Service staff. As a result, we propose to modify the statutory power to grant bail so that it may additionally be exercised by staff outside the Immigration Service.

VOLUNTARY ASSISTED RETURNS

4.85   The voluntary assisted returns programme is a means by which we assist asylum seekers who wish to return home to do so. Asylum seekers are eligible for the programme at any stage of their claim unless they are to be deported or have been granted indefinite leave to enter or remain.

4.86   The programme, which is operated for the Home Office by the International Organisation for Migration (IOM) and Refugee Action, returns people in an orderly, sustainable, and cost effective manner. Through its non-political nature and extensive network of humanitarian NGOs, it has the ability to return people to nearly all countries where it is safe to do so. In the longer term, this establishment of routes to countries where, currently, few exist will assist in removal by the Home Office of those people who are not in need of protection.

4.87   We propose to build on the programme's success using forthcoming legislation to increase its return capability, and also to facilitate early access to the programme through the new Induction and Accommodation Centres.

4.88   Currently, 43% of those applying under this programme seek assistance from IOM before their claim for asylum has been determined. We will enable those who would access it to do so early in the asylum process, thereby further increasing its cost effectiveness.

4.89   We will also continue to work in close partnership with the NGO community and IOM to ensure that the returns are sustainable. Reintegration assistance will be provided to returnees in the form of skills training, employment advice, tools, or the availability of micro-credit schemes. Such assistance will enable our tracking of returnees to ensure their safety and the integrity of the programme.

Refugee Integration

4.90   A key element of the United Kingdom's commitment to be a safe haven for those fleeing persecution is how we help those who have the right to remain here to rebuild their lives and to fulfil their potential as full members of society. There is evidence to suggest that many refugees[18] find it difficult to make the transition from support to independence. Access to services is often low and while new co-ordination measures are in place to improve refugees' access to education, healthcare and employment, difficulties remain.

WORKING IN PARTNERSHIP

4.91   An integration strategy will only be successful if it is built on partnerships. The voluntary sector, central and local government, local service providers, the private sector, refugees and refugee community organisations all have important roles to play. We set out our strategy in November 2000 in *'Full and Equal Citizens – A strategy for the Integration of Refugees into the United Kingdom'*.

4.92   The strategy seeks to learn from the high level of activity and good practice already existing in many areas of the country and in the European Union and elsewhere. It seeks to establish what is effective in integration so that what works can be spread further to other areas and to other communities. Integration is not a mechanistic process. Our aim is not to produce a package into which successful asylum seekers are pushed in at one end and out of which integrated refugees appear at the other. Communities are different. Refugees are different. Our aim is to help all refugees develop their potential and to contribute to the cultural and economic life of the country as equal members of society.

18 In this section, the term 'refugee' applies to recognised refugees who are granted indefinite leave to remain within the terms of the 1951 Convention on the Status of Refugees or those given four years exceptional leave to remain as persons in need of protection in accordance with obligations under the ECHR and the Convention against Torture.

NATIONAL REFUGEE INTEGRATION FORUM

4.93   We are taking forward the integration agenda through the National Refugee Integration Forum, led by the Home Office Minister of State, Lord Rooker. It draws together local authorities, Government departments and the voluntary and private sectors to monitor and steer the development of a strategy for integration. The Forum will be responsible for developing an agreed framework of indicators to find the key elements in a successful integration package. Similar arrangements are being put in place in Scotland.

4.94   The Government's commitment to the Forum is demonstrated through the leadership of Lord Rooker and of Iain Gray in Scotland. But we are clear that we do not hold all of the expertise. The Forum does much of its work through its 9 sub groups, each (except that on research) chaired by a person from outside of central Government who has particular knowledge and expertise of their area and who can, with the help of a very wide range of members, drive forward the agenda in their area.

THE WORK OF THE FORUM

4.95   The Forum contains a number of groups to cover the areas which are clearly recognised as those needing particular attention if barriers to integration are to be overcome:

- Accommodation.
- Community development.
- Community safety and racial harassment.
- Education of children.
- Employment and training.
- Health and social care.
- Positive images.
- Research.
- Unaccompanied asylum seeking children.

4.96   In the first year of its operation, the Forum has identified the key barriers and established much of what needs to be done to remove those barriers. The stage is now set to move from discussion of what the problems are to putting in place the solutions.

PRACTICAL SOLUTIONS

4.97   Some solutions will happen quickly. The Health and Social Care sub group is establishing a website which will give healthcare professionals easy access to material about the special needs of refugees and also to material in a number of key languages. They will share information on how to make sure a refugee who does not speak much English can do a simple thing like understand the instructions on a bottle of prescription medicine. The Community Safety and Racial Harassment group plans to circulate examples of best practice on helping to create safe communities.

4.98   The Employment, Training and Adult Education sub group is looking at the particular difficulties faced by refugees trying to enter the job market. The group is considering data on the profile of refugee jobseekers, recognition of overseas qualifications, the promotion of employment amongst employers and consultation with the Department for Work and Pensions (DWP) to develop a policy on refugee employment. As part of its wider strategy, the Department for Education and Skills (DfES) has already identified the need for a new curriculum for the teaching of ESOL. English language is a vital skill for refugee job-seekers and an important tool for successful integration. We will continue to work on the development of effective programmes in this area

4.99   Recognised refugees in need of ESOL tuition are already able to access New Deal provision. Take-up of this however can be low and this may be due in part to the particular needs and circumstances of refugees. The National Forum will be working closely with DfES and DWP to ensure that the new curriculum operates in a way which benefits refugees and the skills they bring.

4.100   The Government will publish a more detailed account of the Forum's work in April setting out the way forward in all these areas.

4.101   We are also keen to explore how we can develop effective mentoring schemes that can assist refugees to settle successfully in the UK. Such schemes can be effective in helping refugees find and sustain suitable housing, improve their language skills, find employment, make positive links with the wider community and understand the culture and values of the host country. Some work on befriending refugees does already take place in the UK but is more developed elsewhere, for example, in Canada, where refugees can be helped with the process of integration. Such models recognise that integration is a two-way process, in which both refugee and host community have a role, and can contribute towards stronger more cohesive communities. Many British people will want to act as mentors to newly arrived refugees, or help those seeking to acquire citizenship, to learn about British society. As part of its wider agenda for civil renewal, the Government will promote volunteering opportunities for people who want to help in this way – through, for example, the newly launched Experience Corps, Timebank and local volunteer bureaux.

FUNDING

4.102   Our strategy also established 3 wholly new streams of funding for integration issues. At the same time, additional funds to be administered by the United Kingdom through the European Refugee Fund became available:

- £650,000 has been given to voluntary sector agencies to support ongoing community development so that refugees, wherever they have been accommodated across the UK, can have access to support from local community groups. This was an important element of the dispersal process and there are already many indicators of increased activity amongst community groups. The Government wants local communities to be strong and is keen to see this development continue.
- £350,000 is being made available each year through the Refugee Community Development Fund. This fund is providing small amounts of seed corn funding for small community groups who are making their first steps towards working with refugees. It enables translation of material to encourage refugee women to join local groups and the purchase of computers. Integration needs to have a strong base in local communities and this fund will provide some of that support.
- The key fund is the Challenge Fund. Originally established at £500,000 per year, the Government announced in November that this will be doubled to £1 million per year from April 2002. Together with the integration strand of the European Refugee Fund, the money is being used to fund projects in the main integration areas such as improving the access to the labour market and housing.

4.103   But it is not just funding projects alone. What the Fund is doing is testing and monitoring these projects to the full so that we can test to the limits what it is that really works in integration. We are setting out to compare what one English language course can deliver that another does not. We want to see whether other factors are involved. We want to know if there is a regional difference in what works. We want to know what refugees find most effective. This is a real opportunity not just for the Government but for those involved in delivering the projects on the ground. We are providing advice and technical support so that projects have the capacity to cope with this extensive monitoring and to help them build better projects for the future.

4.104   This is an important initiative which will for the first time provide a national base of properly evaluated, fully recorded best practice which we will be able to share across the UK.

4.105   A national approach to integration is a new concept for the UK and we are at the beginning of the process. But the Government is committed to integration as a vital part of the whole asylum process and is determined to give those who qualify as refugees every possible opportunity to build their lives here as full and equal citizens.

Chapter 5

TACKLING FRAUD – PEOPLE TRAFFICKING, ILLEGAL ENTRY AND ILLEGAL WORKING

Organised immigration crime

5.1   We have set out in previous chapters how the Government intends to allow controlled, orderly migration of people who can make a positive contribution to society. We have also set out how we are opening alternative, legal routes for those wishing to work in the UK. However, the Government is determined to prevent this system from being undermined by people coming illegally to the UK or working here in breach of the law. We will tackle the organised criminals who cynically and systematically attempt to evade the controls and we are determined to prevent, detect and deal with illegal working within the UK by those who slip through the net.

Nature and Scale of the Problem

5.2   The vast majority of people who arrive in the UK illegally are brought here by organised crime groups. This organised immigration crime includes both 'people trafficking', where someone is brought to the UK in order to be exploited, and 'people smuggling' where, at least to some extent, entry is facilitated with their consent. It is best seen as a range of closely related phenomena, set out in more detail in the box. Whilst exact figures are impossible to judge, available evidence points to the majority of illegal immigrants to the UK being here by their consent and that the number of trafficked people is small by comparison.

People smuggling is the facilitation of illegal entry; entering the UK in breach of immigration law, either secretly or through deception. Those who are smuggled are invariably complicit and are effectively customers availing themselves of the smugglers' services. This can be a simple business transaction between the criminal and the illegal entrant. But in other cases, the criminal deceives their customer by exaggerating their prospects in the UK and demands a very high price. The customer may spend their life savings on a dangerous journey that merely leads to their immediate removal.

People trafficking is transporting people in order to exploit them, using deception, intimidation or coercion. Those who can truly be described as trafficking victims have usually been treated as little more than a commodity. The exploitation may take the form of bonded labour or servitude which violates their legal or human rights. It may be commercial sexual exploitation. It is often accompanied by violence, or threats of violence, against the victim or their family. The victim may agree to a deal which includes entry into the UK and work on arrival. They then find that their wages are largely diverted to pay off 'debts' to the criminals, and that they have been deceived as to the nature and conditions of the work. Trafficking usually involves a breach of immigration law – either illegal entry, or overstaying. When it does, it can make the victim more vulnerable because they are reluctant to seek help.

Illegal working in this context is working by people who are in the UK illegally, or by those in the UK legally who have no right to work here.

Exploitation – whether of illegal or other workers – is harmful, not only for the victim, but also undermines our National Minimum Wage and labour standards. Both people trafficking and smuggling usually involve illegal working, and trafficking always involves exploitation. So successful action against illegal working and exploitation is not only desirable in itself, but will also reduce incentives for organised criminals to bring people to the UK.

5.3 There are no reliable estimates of the scale of organised immigration crime within the UK or EU as a whole. One indication of the scale of the problem is the number of people detected trying to evade border controls. This has risen from 3,300 in 1990 to over 47,000 in 2000 – although this partly reflects the increasing effectiveness of the Immigration Service. It is estimated that organised criminals were behind around 75% of these cases. It is unknown how many involved, or would have involved, exploitation. Home Office research in 2000[19]

19 'Stopping Traffic: exploring the extent of and response to trafficking in women for sexual exploitation in the UK': Liz Kelly and Linda Regan (Police Research Series Paper 125) May 2000.

estimated that somewhere between 150 and 1500 women annually are trafficked into the UK for the purpose of sexual exploitation, although this was a rough estimate. Further research is in progress which may shed more light on the size and nature of irregular immigrant flows through Europe into the UK and on the reasons why people decide to come illegally to the UK.

5.4   Organised immigration crime is a complex problem, and we are determined to address every aspect of it – in countries of origin, en route to the UK and on arrival. It requires co-ordination across Government Departments; partnership with business and voluntary sectors; and international co-operation. Our strategy focuses on:

- Combating illegal working: improved enforcement action, less potential for fraud, effective gathering and sharing of information and working with business.
- Strengthening the law.
- Dealing appropriately with victims of trafficking;
- Tackling the criminals: intelligence and enforcement operations.
- EU co-operation.
- Prevention in source and transit countries.

Illegal Working

5.5   It is clear that people who are in this country illegally are vulnerable to exploitation both by the traffickers that use deception or intimidation to transport them and by a few unscrupulous employers or gangmasters who take advantage of their status by making them work in poor or dangerous conditions, often for unacceptably low wages. People in this situation can be too afraid to challenge their treatment yet powerless to escape their exploiters. Because of their status, many illegal migrants are socially excluded and have few opportunities to make a positive contribution to the community.

5.6   However, the problems are far more wide-ranging than this. Some of these employers are paying their workers below the minimum wage. They may also avoid other employer responsibilities, such as welfare provision, safety requirements or paying tax and National Insurance contributions. But they are not only exploiting the workers, such employers are also gaining an unfair advantage over legitimate businesses driving legitimate employers out of business.

5.7   The apparent availability of illicit work, even where it is at the expense of legitimate business, acts as a pull factor for more would-be migrants. Whilst the Government must take the lead, we **all** have a responsibility – Government, business and the public – to ensure that illegal work is not readily available in the UK. It has to be clear to those who seek work here that we are tackling this issue and that there are alternative legitimate routes. Managed migration schemes and our wider employment policies will help to ensure that labour market demands can be met through legal sources and that those wishing to work in the UK have legal routes available to them. Those who facilitate the illegal entry of people to the UK or harbour them once here – be they employers or not – need to understand that they are committing a very serious offence, which will in future carry a potential 14 year prison sentence. Using the Proceeds of Crime Bill, those who profit from this crime will also face the prospect of losing those profits.

Scale of the problem

5.8   For the purposes of this White Paper the focus is on illegal migrant workers. This refers to migrants who are present in the UK illegally and to those who are here lawfully but have no right to work. By its very nature, the scale of illegal employment is extremely difficult to measure. While there are no accurate means of estimating the numbers involved, the most reliable indicators suggest that the number could run into hundreds of thousands.

5.9   The problem is particularly severe where the availability of work is greatest. It is therefore unsurprising that lower wage employment sectors, such as catering, cleaning and hospitality, are particularly affected. Other sectors are also disproportionately affected, such as the construction industry and seasonal employment areas including agriculture. But the problem is not limited exclusively to these areas.

Current practice

5.10   Section 8 of the Asylum and Immigration Act 1996, made it an offence for employers knowingly or negligently to employ people who have no permission to work. The maximum penalty that can be imposed on an employer if the offence is proved is £5,000 for each illegal employee. Employers can establish a defence by proving that they were shown one of a number of documents showing entitlement to work and that they believed this to be genuine. Documents currently specified are wide-ranging.

5.11   These measures have not proved to be an effective deterrent[20]. The reasons for this are numerous but the Government is aware that employers are often confused about their duties and unclear as to how to verify employment status, particularly as fraudulent documents are not uncommon and, although successful joint operations have been mounted, to date, this has not been an exemplar of 'joined up' government.

A new approach

5.12   We are determined to put the situation right and tackle the problem of illegal working in the UK. But, as explained above, this issue cannot be looked at in isolation. Reflecting the importance and cross-cutting nature of the problem, a Ministerial Working Group was established last year. This Group, which was announced by the Home Secretary in October 2001, is chaired by Home Office Minister of State, Lord Rooker. It includes representatives from a number of Government Departments.

5.13   Tackling illegal working sits alongside the policies of managed migration, measures to tackle organised crime, wider labour market policies, and the issues of social exclusion, integration and citizenship. It is therefore necessary to take a holistic approach, ensuring that proposals benefit individuals, business and wider society.

5.14   While unscrupulous employers believe that employing illegal migrants, rather than domestic workers or legal migrants, offers benefits that far outweigh the risks, they will continue to flout the law. And while these illegal work opportunities continue to exist, the phenomenon of people being smuggled and trafficked to this country and exploited, or simply coming here, quite legally, but then working illegally, will continue.

5.15   There is no simple answer. Many nations across the world have put in place measures designed to prevent or limit illegal working. It is important to learn from the experience of others while remaining aware that each nation is unique. What the Government proposes will address the situation here.

---

20 The number of people prosecuted successfully under Section 8 of the Asylum and Immigration Act 1996 since 1997 are: 0 in 1997; 1 in 1998; 9 in 1998; 23 in 2000 (provisional).

New measures

5.16   To tackle the damaging consequences of illegal working, we need to address the root of the problem. That is why there will be action in source countries and firm action on people traffickers and smugglers. It also means targeting employers as well as individuals who are knowingly working illegally, recognising, of course, that some of these people are victims. Where workers have no right to be in the UK, they can expect to be removed. As outlined earlier, we recognise that legal routes can help to meet the demand and we will continue to build on the work of the New Deal and other measures being taken forward by the Department for Work and Pensions.

5.17   The Government intends to ensure that present enforcement arrangements are strengthened by:

- Reducing scope for fraud by limiting the range of identification acceptable as evidence of Section 8 compliance. For asylum seekers, replacing the present paper based Standard Acknowledgement Letter with an Application Registration Card which will provide much better protection against forgery and counterfeiting and allow fast verification of identity.
- Improving the enforcement capacity and capability of the Immigration Service, to make tackling illegal working a higher priority and developing joint Immigration Service and police teams with specialist skills to target illegal working.
- Mounting joint operations to tackle illegal working and other workplace offences.
- Using the Proceeds of Crime Bill to remove the profits of those who exploit illegal working for their own advantage.
- Making it clear that the new penalties for facilitating people smuggling will apply to **all** those who facilitate the illegal entry of migrants and assist in hiding those who are here.
- Improving security of the National Insurance Number (NINO). The Enhanced NINO Process, introduced nationally from April 2001, ensures a consistent approach for establishing the identity of all adults seeking NINO registration.

5.18   In performing its law enforcement functions, the Immigration and Nationality Directorate requires information from various other sources to enable it to combat fraud, people trafficking and illegal employment and to locate offenders. The Government is considering whether the powers currently possessed by the Immigration and Nationality Directorate and the Joint Entry Clearance Unit in this important area are adequate to meet the challenges of the early 21st Century. We will decide whether they should be strengthened in the forthcoming legislation. We are examining the degree to which more information might be shared within

Government, taking into account the work of the Cabinet Office Performance and Innovation Unit on data sharing, Lord Grabiner's recommendations following his investigation into the informal economy and the degree to which information might be required from a broader range of social players. There is clearly a vital balance to be struck here between the rights of individuals to privacy on the one hand and the wider needs of society on the other. In reaching decisions on these matters, we will take this fully into account.

5.19   Finally, the Government intends to work with business and trades unions to improve compliance by:

- Producing and promoting guidance to support Section 8 compliance.
- Providing support, possibly through an improved telephone helpline.
- Developing industry codes of practice.
- Working closely with the Office of Government Commerce [OGC] to address this issue in the public sector.

5.20   A high-level steering group consisting of representatives of business and the trades unions will be invited to consider these issues and develop innovative solutions.

5.21   Taken together, these measures will send out a strong message of our determination to tackle illegal working. To employers in the UK, the public and internationally, they will be seen as part of the coherent package of proposed asylum and immigration measures. They are a starting point for tackling illegal working, not a panacea to what is a very complex issue. They will be complemented by effective arrangements, including managed migration, to ensure that legal labour is available to satisfy UK business needs. The Government acknowledges that getting the balance right will not be easy. But through these measures, we are getting our own house in order by ensuring that enforcement is effective and simplifying compliance.

ENTITLEMENT CARDS

After the terrorist atrocities in the United States on 11 September, the issue of introducing an identity card scheme was raised by many people and attracted a considerable degree of media comment. At the time, the Government said that it was not planning to introduce an identity card scheme as part of its response to the events of 11 September, but that the policy was being kept under review and that it was considering whether a universal entitlement card, which could allow people to prove their identity more easily and provide a simple way to access a range of public services, would be beneficial. The Government also said that a scheme could help to combat illegal working and it could also reduce fraud against individuals, public services and the private sector.

The Government made clear that the introduction of an entitlement card would be a major step and that it would not proceed without consulting widely and considering all the views expressed very carefully. There are many arguments – both philosophical and practical – for and against a scheme.

One of the options which the Government has already ruled out is making the failure to carry an entitlement card an offence.

However, there are a range of other issues to explore and the Government intends to publish a consultation paper in the spring or early summer. This will cover the whole issue of identity fraud and a range of possible responses in the short, medium and long-term, including the advantages and disadvantages of an entitlement card scheme – but also other measures which might be taken to improve the security of existing forms of identification issued by the Government. The Government wants to see a full debate on the issues around nationality, immigration and citizenship arising from this White Paper and does not want these confused with the broader and separate debate on entitlement cards which is why these issues will be set out in a separate consultation paper. In order to ensure that the paper will be balanced and comprehensive, and present to the public as full a picture as possible, the Government wishes to discuss its emerging ideas with interested parties prior to publication.

The Government will be consulting employers and trade unions on all the issues on ensuring that employers comply with their duty under Section 8 of the Asylum and Immigration Act 1996. The use of entitlement cards to provide a means of identification of potential employees to assist employer compliance with Section 8, and to reduce the opportunities for fraudulent representations by those not entitled to work in the UK, is one option which the Government would like to discuss.

Strengthening the law

5.22   A comprehensive approach to organised immigration crime must include having appropriate legislation. We will send out a clear signal that where criminals seek to bring people into the UK illegally, and exploit them, they will face the full force of the law. People smuggling is already a criminal offence but we will make the law stronger and more effective. We will also be bringing forward detailed legislation to cover people trafficking, both internationally and within this country, as soon as possible. The legislation will cover those being trafficked for both labour and sexual exploitation. But such measures go wider than is possible in immigration legislation. We need to act now to deal with the gross abuse represented by those who traffic people here from abroad for their sexual exploitation. We will therefore use the forthcoming immigration legislation to introduce a new offence of trafficking people from abroad to this country for the purposes of sexual exploitation.

5.23   Effective action in all these areas requires that other countries also have adequate legal frameworks. The UK has been pivotal in negotiating key international measures to tackle organised immigration crime, primarily the UN Protocol on Trafficking[21] and two EU Framework Decisions, one on trafficking and one on the facilitation of illegal entry. Facilitation is the involvement in an activity which assists someone to enter, transit or remain in a Member State contrary to the laws of that country. These measures ensure that throughout the EU, there is a shared legal basis for action against organised immigration crime. In the UK, we will ensure that we have the toughest possible sanctions against the traffickers and smugglers.

NEW LAWS ON PEOPLE SMUGGLING

5.24   We will be using forthcoming immigration legislation to strengthen the law on people smuggling. The offence of facilitating illegal entry currently carries a maximum penalty of 10 years' imprisonment. We propose to increase it to match the 14 year maximum for many drug trafficking offences, which is significantly higher than the 8 years recommended by the EU Framework Decision on the facilitation of illegal entry. The law will also penalise those who attempt to benefit from people smuggling, even if they have not been directly involved in it, or who help immigration offenders to remain here unlawfully.

5.25   We will ensure that the law enables the removal of people who arrive here legally but then try to rely on deception or forged documents in an attempt to obtain further leave. We will also make it an offence to possess counterfeit endorsing stamps of the kind used to grant leave to enter or remain.

21 Protocol to prevent, suppress and punish trafficking in persons, especially women and children, supplementing the UN Convention against Transnational Organised Crime (2000).

5.26   We will take powers to bring children born in the UK, where both parents are illegal entrants or while the family is on temporary admission, into the immigration process at an earlier stage so that the current absence of such powers cannot be used to delay the family's removal.

NEW LAWS ON TRAFFICKING FOR SEXUAL EXPLOITATION

5.27   This unacceptable crime was covered by a comprehensive review of the law on sex offences which the Government published in July 2000[22].Amongst its recommendations was a proposed new offence of trafficking for the purpose of commercial sexual exploitation.

5.28   Existing laws already cover this area but they are out of date and the penalties generally are low. Following responses to public consultation, we are considering what changes to the law are necessary to strengthen the legal framework for tackling these evils. We intend to bring forward wide-ranging changes to the law to deal with trafficking for commercial sexual exploitation both domestically and internationally. In the short-term, however, we are determined to close the loophole that allows foreign and EU nationals of whatever sex or age to be brought to the UK for the purposes of sexual exploitation. We will use the forthcoming immigration legislation to introduce a new offence of trafficking for the purposes of sexual exploitation as a stopgap pending the major reform. This will carry a heavy maximum penalty of 14 years' imprisonment.

NEW LAWS ON TRAFFICKING FOR LABOUR EXPLOITATION

5.29   This aspect of trafficking involves moving a person or persons from one location to another for the purposes of exploiting their labour and is often carried out by the use of force, fraud or coercion.

5.30   Trafficking for labour exploitation not only penalises the direct victims but also works against the competitiveness of decent employers who comply with employment law. We will strengthen our means of tackling this problem by introducing legislation which will make trafficking of people for the purposes of labour exploitation a specific criminal offence.

22 'Setting the Boundaries – reforming the law on sex offences', Home Office, July 2000.

Victims of exploitation

5.31   People arriving in the UK illegally form a disparate group. Some are willing customers; a few, particularly those working as prostitutes, are brought to the UK and forcibly exploited to provide labour or services. We need to offer such victims particular support so that they can escape their circumstances and recognise they may be able to help law enforcement against organised criminals.

5.32   Where such people are willing to come forward to the authorities, we shall, where necessary, make special arrangements for their protection. We must acknowledge that if they do co-operate with the authorities, they may risk reprisals against themselves or their loved ones in their own countries. We will consider, in the light of individual circumstances, whether it would be appropriate to allow them to remain here. But, if they are not entitled to remain here, and it is not appropriate to let them stay, they must be returned to their own country wherever possible. To do otherwise would undermine the UK's immigration law and open the door for traffickers to exploit more victims. But we will assist them to return by providing them with initial counselling, ensuring they have suitable accommodation to return to and helping them to reintegrate into their own community and find employment.

5.33   We will work with the voluntary sector to put the necessary arrangements in place. This initiative will run on a trial basis for 6 months in the first place so that we can evaluate its impact.

5.34   So our approach needs to:

   • Identify the victims of serious crimes and offer them the care and support they need.
   • Facilitate the disruption and prosecution of organised crime by making the most of information they can give us and allowing them to act as witnesses, where appropriate.
   • Ensure that if not entitled to stay in the UK, they are successfully removed wherever possible.
   • Send out a clear message that illegal immigration to the UK does not pay.

5.35   The Government will develop this approach further. Parts of the Police and Immigration Service already apply it. We intend to develop a best practice 'toolkit' to help those who deal with illegal immigrants and trafficking victims to distinguish victims in genuine need and to deal with them appropriately. This toolkit will be important for practitioners, chiefly police and immigration officers, who will use it to identify victims and ensure that the right procedures are followed to provide the victims with the support and help they need. It will be a comprehensive summary of best practice based on 'what works'.

Tackling the criminals: intelligence and enforcement operations

5.36   In 2000, the Government set up Project Reflex, a multi-agency task force chaired by the National Crime Squad (NCS). Its remit is to co-ordinate operations against trafficking and smuggling and to develop the intelligence and strategic planning to underpin them. It brings together all the agencies involved in combating trafficking, such as the NCS, the National Criminal Intelligence Service (NCIS), the Immigration Service (IS), the Foreign & Commonwealth Office, the Intelligence and Security Agencies, and key police forces including the Metropolitan Police, Kent and the British Transport Police.

5.37   Under Reflex, a central tasking forum has been established to plan and co-ordinate multi-agency operations. It is now well established and has resulted in some major successes involving partners overseas:

Operation Franc targeted a major network smuggling Turkish nationals. Over a 2-year period, the Immigration Service, NCIS and the police built up a picture of an extensive, well-organised gang with contacts throughout Western Europe. Disruptive action, in highly effective co-operation with the French, disabled several small-time operatives and caught hundreds of illegal entrants on both sides of the Channel. In a final strike, both the leader of the gang and his lieutenant were arrested, together with five other gang members. They are now awaiting trial.

Operation Zephaniah broke up a racket which arranged the entry of hundreds of illegal entrants from Northern India over a 2-year period. It was run mainly through Dover, using hired vans and a pool of casual drivers. The enforcement operation was international, involving a number of UK agencies, including the Immigration Service, Customs and the police, and the German Border Police. It resulted in the arrest of the ringleaders, both in Germany and the UK, and the seizure of false passports and documentation and a large quantity of 'bootleg' alcohol and cigarettes. The main organiser was sentenced to 6 years' imprisonment.

Operation Mullet was a major enquiry, conducted by the Immigration Service with Leicester Police, into a band of conspirators facilitating illegal entry using forged documentation. The main forger was so good that his services were in demand by other criminal gangs. He used UK passports stolen from the houses of Asian families in Leicester. Eight people were arrested, including the forger and the main ringleader, and all received long prison sentences.

5.38   We have also established a joint Immigration Service and National Crime Squad unit to lead investigations against those involved in serious organised immigration crime. This is now fully operational. Its intelligence capacity will include specialist financial investigators and a unit for handling informants. Surveillance teams will comprise both NCS and IS staff trained to the same standards. It will also provide legal assistance to investigations.

5.39   Effective operations depend on effective use of intelligence – gathering and analysing it and sharing it between agencies. The Reflex intelligence strategy has been based around building up a comprehensive assessment of the nature and scale of organised immigration crime, identifying knowledge gaps to be filled and a detailed analysis of trafficking routes and key 'nexus points' through which gangs recruit and transport migrants.

EU co-operation

5.40   Organised criminal groups do not respect national boundaries, and immigration crime is international. Effective action against it therefore requires close co-operation with other countries, particularly with our EU partners. The UK is fully signed up to work under EU funding programmes to help Member States, source and transit countries to tackle immigration crime through a wide range of preventative measures and by operational co-operation. The European Council at Tampere set out an agenda for tackling illegal immigration, especially people trafficking. The UK welcomes the progress already made, including the Directive on Smuggling and the two Framework Decisions on Smuggling and Trafficking mentioned above. A recent European Commission Communication on a Common Policy on Illegal Immigration calls for increased co-operation with both source and transit countries and practical implementation and efficient enforcement of existing rules aimed at preventing illegal immigration. It also proposes an Action Plan covering visa policy, information exchange, border management, police co-operation, legislative action and returns policy.

5.41   We are working closely with the Commission, the Presidency of the EU and other Member States to build upon and then implement the broad range of measures the Action Plan proposes.

5.42   Another main area where a co-operative approach is needed is on returning illegal immigrants once they are apprehended. The UK is already involved in some successful returns programmes covering a range of countries and has been negotiating bilateral agreements with others. We will work to expand co-operation on returns, both bilaterally and by seeking to develop a joined up EU approach.

5.43　But co-operation on policy is only half the story. Collaborative operations are equally important. This includes action like Operations Zephania and Franc, mentioned above, where we work with one other country. It also includes, where appropriate, operations involving many countries such as the EU High Impact Operation in autumn 2001. This was a joint initiative with EU applicant countries to tackle illegal immigration across the future eastern borders of the EU. The UK would like to see a wider use of one-off, high impact operations targeting weak border points and key transit routes, creating a maximum deterrent effect. These will be most effective under a flexible, multi-lateral approach, in which different groups of countries participate according to operational requirements. We will work with our EU partners to develop this approach.

5.44　The UK is also developing a network of Immigration Liaison Officers (ILOs), working with other governments to encourage and support action to disrupt the activities of criminal gangs and create a joint intelligence structure. ILOs have recently started work in Zagreb, Rome, Vienna and Budapest. Five more are expected to be in place in Turkey, Belgrade, Sofia, Kiev and Warsaw by April 2002. ILOs within other EU countries have proved very valuable and we are considering the case for an extension of this work. All UK ILOs form part of the wider emerging EU ILO network, guidelines for which were adopted in May 2001. The guidelines will help co-ordination of activity and sharing of intelligence.

Prevention in source and transit countries

5.45　As mentioned above, a comprehensive approach to people trafficking and smuggling must also include prevention in countries of origin. The primary aim is to stop organised illegal immigration into the UK. But most people trafficking takes place between other countries. The most abusive forms of it, in which the victims are often women and children, are more prevalent outside the UK. It is right that many of our prevention activities also help to reduce trafficking outside the UK. Prevention has three elements:

- Addressing the causes of emigration.
- Helping potential migrants avoid deception and coercion.
- Technical assistance to governments to help prevent organised crime.

5.46　If we wish to have a significant and lasting effect on organised immigration crime, we must also address the factors which make people vulnerable to exploitation such as poverty, war and repression. We must prevent traffickers from taking advantage of others' desperation to move. We need to support the efforts of developing countries to promote economic growth and social development , eliminate poverty, improve governance and reduce conflict. Tackling these underlying factors will also promote social justice, for example by encouraging core labour standards banning forced and bonded labour or child labour; and creating opportunities for women, who are at far greater risk of being trafficked than men, particularly for sexual exploitation.

5.47   Another strand in our strategy for addressing the root causes of organised immigration crime is raising awareness through public information initiatives of its perils in source and transit countries. We are ensuring that we inform potential victims about the dangers of being trafficked or smuggled and that they have full, undistorted information on whether they can legally enter the UK and what their employment and other prospects would be on arrival.

5.48   Governments in many source and transit countries lack the resources, infrastructure or awareness to take effective preventative action against organised criminals. The UK can offer assistance by:

- Ensuring their officials can recognise outgoing people at risk of being trafficked, especially at borders, and offer them help.
- Developing an appropriate legal framework and enforcing the law to deal with organised criminals on their own soil.
- Effective reintegration of returned migrants so they are not trafficked or smuggled again.
- Helping to reduce corruption, which may hinder some countries' attempts to deal with organised crime.

5.49   The UK, through the Department for International Development and the Foreign and Commonwealth Office, already funds a range of projects in source and transit countries which offer assistance in all four of these areas. Some of these are collaborative ventures with other countries and with international organisations. A few examples are given in the box below. We are encouraging and supporting states in implementing the UN Protocol on Trafficking which provides a template for co-ordinated international action to suppress and punish trafficking.

EXAMPLE - PREVENTATIVE PROJECTS

An example of tackling trafficking between developing countries is a project by the International Programme on the Elimination of Child Labour (IPEC), partly funded by DfID, to combat the trafficking of children within the **Mekong** subregion. This has been expanded and now aims more broadly at reducing labour exploitation of women and children, through targeting trafficking.

Many illegal migrants and trafficking victims pass through the **Balkans** en route to the EU and the UK. A number of projects focus on this key transit region.

- The Prime Minister's Balkans initiative has sent teams of immigration experts from several EU Member States to work along the State Border Service in Bosnia-Herzegovina, training, advising and helping them to develop their legal and administrative infrastructure to deal with illegal entry.
- The Balkan Stability Pact's Migration and Asylum Initiative (MAI) and Anti-Trafficking Task Force (ATTF). The UK has agreed to support the MAI as a partner to Bosnia and is involved in the establishment of the ATTF. The objective of the initiative is to bring the asylum and migration systems of five Balkans countries (Yugoslavia, Croatia, Bosnia Herzegovina, Albania and Macedonia) as close as possible to EU standards.

Chapter 6

BORDER CONTROLS

6.1   The challenges posed by today's immigration control are immense, reflecting the UK's status as a major centre of international trade and travel. The Government's aim is to ensure that genuine visitors and others who have a right to be here pass as quickly as possible through the Immigration Control. However, we also need to tackle the ever-present problem of individuals and organisations who seek to circumvent the control. We will do this by targeting the problem of illegal migration at source and building on the achievements already made.

6.2   The increase in international travel has meant that the number of persons found inadmissible to the UK and removed has doubled, from an annual figure of 19,180 in 1990 to 38,275 in 2000. We have been working hard to ensure that those who do not claim asylum but who are here illegally, often working without permission to do so, are removed from the UK when apprehended. We removed 5,254 such offenders from April 2000 to March 2001. Over the same period, immigration officers detected 34,138 people on arrival who did not qualify for admission under the Immigration Rules and were refused entry and removed. We must continue to ensure that passengers who have no claim to come here are prevented from doing so. In order to achieve this goal, the Immigration and Nationality Directorate has implemented a number of important initiatives. The Government intends to maintain the effort devoted to these areas and investigate new ways of tackling large numbers of unfounded asylum claims and the use of forged and stolen documents.

6.3   One of the paradoxes of publicity around those desperate to get across the Channel into the United Kingdom is the fact that so many of them are unable to do so. The steps taken over recent years to tighten controls at Channel ports has led to the build up of those attempting to get through the Channel tunnel and the scenes at Sangatte, the rail freight terminal at Frethun and the Coquelles facility itself. We also know the problem exists further afield, with more sophisticated attempts being made to board freight trains bound for Britain. We will continue to work with hauliers and other transport operators to ensure they take responsibility for the security of their vehicles on transport links into the UK. As indicated elsewhere, legitimate gateways for refugees seeking asylum from outside the country are an important new step in rationalising and controlling those in desperate need. But rigorous prevention of the breach of border controls remains a critical element in building up confidence and trust and sending the appropriate signals to both traffickers and potential clandestine migrants. We need to maintain close co-operation with our European partners, in particular our colleagues in France, with whom we share deep concerns about the issue of cross-Channel illegal immigration.

6.4   The Government will build on our successes so far and develop new initiatives using the latest technology. We will:

- Continue to deploy our network of Airline Liaison Officers stationed overseas to help prevent improperly documented passengers travelling to the UK.
- Continue to use visa regimes for nationals of countries where there is evidence of the systematic abuse of our controls.
- Continue to deploy immigration officers abroad where this is necessary to check passengers before they travel to the UK.
- Maintain our new operational arrangements for UK immigration officers conducting immigration controls in France.
- Develop a new concept of screening passengers before they travel to the UK whereby they are checked against IND databases to confirm their eligibility to travel.
- Develop the use of biometric technology, for example, iris or facial recognition and fingerprints , for use in expediting the clearance of particular categories of passenger, whilst at the same time safeguarding these passengers from identity abuse by others.
- Utilise x/gamma ray scanners and CCTV to help locate those seeking to enter illegally, whilst evaluating the latest technology using thermal imaging and acoustic sensors to detect those concealed in vehicles and containers.
- Use mobile task forces as part of an intelligence-led control.
- Work together with European partners, candidate and other countries to strengthen the EU's common border and enhance border controls on transit routes.

Airline Liaison Officers

6.5   The Airline Liaison Officer (ALO) network has continued to provide essential and invaluable support to the immigration control. Since 1993, when the UK posted its first ALO abroad, the network has expanded and there are now ALOs based in twenty locations around the world. Our carriers' liability legislation places the onus on carriers to check that passengers are properly documented for travel to the UK. ALOs work in partnership with airlines abroad, offering advice on the acceptability of documents presented for travel. They do so by frequently attending flight departures at overseas airports to give on the spot advice and through an extensive programme of formal training for airline staff in UK passport and visa requirements, as well as in forgery awareness. During 2001, 22,515 inadequately documented passengers en route to the UK and elsewhere were denied boarding by carriers at ALO locations. This represents a significant success for the network in stemming the flow of improperly documented passengers to the UK, which we intend to support and maintain. The Government is committed to playing a full part in the EU's action to improve the co-ordination of European ALO activities and enhance their training programmes.

Visa Regimes

6.6   Visa regimes represent an effective tool in the control of those seeking to come to the UK. A visa regime will normally be imposed where there is evidence of the systematic abuse of our immigration controls by the nationals of a particular country. Those people who are subject to a visa regime must satisfy the same requirements as non-visa nationals, but must do so before travelling to the UK rather than at the port on arrival. At present the nationals of 110 countries or territories must have a visa if they wish to visit the UK.

6.7   The Government is committed to ensuring that all those who have a genuine reason to come to the UK are able to do so with as little inconvenience as possible. For this reason, the visa process has been developed so that the issue of a visa is combined with the grant of leave to enter before the passenger has travelled. Entry may still be refused in certain circumstances, but the vast majority of visa holders may pass swiftly through the immigration control after a brief check of their documents on arrival.

Pre – Clearance

6.8   Visa regimes are not always appropriate, however, so we are examining new ways in which those travelling to the UK can be examined before they embark. One such initiative has been the introduction of pre-clearance, a system that allows UK officials to carry out immigration checks at airports abroad on passengers seeking to come to the UK. We have successfully introduced pre-clearance at Prague airport in the Czech Republic.

6.9   The Czech Republic and UK are close friends and NATO allies. Both Governments are strongly committed to the highest standards of human rights for all their citizens. We were both therefore concerned at the large numbers – more than 1,200 in the first half of 2001 – of inadmissible Czech citizens arriving in the UK, many of whom applied for asylum. On 9 February 2001, therefore, the Czech and British Governments entered into an agreement which allows British Embassy Consular Officers in Prague to pre-clear all passengers boarding flights to the UK. Since 18 July 2001, pre-clearance has been successfully carried out in short phases, varying from several days to weeks at a time. This has proved to be an effective way of tackling the problem of inadmissible passengers travelling direct from Prague airport to the UK. It sends a clear message that the UK is determined to increase the effectiveness of our overseas controls and to disrupt the activities and travel of those involved in organised abuse of UK immigration laws. We shall continue to deploy the scheme flexibly, in co-operation with the Czech Government, in response to operational needs. We will also look for other opportunities to use similar schemes elsewhere.

Juxtaposed Control

6.10   For more than two years, Eurostar services from France have been targeted by persons intending to arrive in the UK either without documents or with forged or stolen documents. We have been working in close co-operation with the French authorities to close off this major loophole in the immigration control. In June last year, we established a system whereby immigration officers from the UK operate a passport control at French stations serving the Eurostar – known as juxtaposed controls. The benefits of this have been dramatic. Since the introduction of the new arrangements the numbers of improperly documented passengers arriving by Eurostar from France have fallen by 75% on the same period in 2000.

6.11   The French authorities have recently passed legislation which introduces a number of measures to strengthen the control over persons seeking to travel illegally to the UK. The legislation ensures that all passengers travelling on the Eurostar trains, whatever their destination, must go through UK immigration controls before boarding. In addition, the train operator in France must inform all passengers that they require documents if they intend to travel to the UK. Furthermore, all persons boarding Eurostar trains are deemed to be seeking to arrive in the UK through the Tunnel system, regardless of whether their ticket indicates a French or UK destination. These measures should close an important loophole in our joint procedures.

Authority to Carry

6.12   We believe we should build on the successes of visa regimes, the ALO network, juxtaposed control and pre-clearance to strengthen further the controls we operate abroad. This is essential so that we can continue to operate an effective immigration control despite the likely increase in the overall number of passengers travelling to the UK in the future. In order to meet the challenges of a modern immigration control, we intend to add to the improvements we have already made to our flexibility, efficiency and effectiveness. We have been looking at the process that a passenger follows when travelling to the UK. We want to see how we can enhance our relations with carriers and other stakeholders and make greater use of technology in the control of passengers.

6.13   We have therefore been developing ideas including an 'Authority to Carry' concept that would allow carriers to check the details of passengers against Home Office databases and receive instant confirmation that they pose no known security or immigration threat. A feasibility study will be undertaken this spring with a view to developing a scheme that could be rolled out shortly after that and in conjunction with carriers and other stakeholders.

6.14   The use of modern technology provides an opportunity for carriers to check and receive instant confirmation that they are free to carry the passenger to the UK. This will provide reassurance that those who are known to pose a threat to the UK will not be able to travel here. Authority to Carry will not replace the other measures detailed above or the controls carried out at UK ports but will complement them by providing another tool in the management of those travelling to the UK. Knowing that passengers have been cleared through the Authority to Carry scheme will also allow the Immigration Service to target its resources better at areas of high risk. This in turn will have benefits for travellers who will pass more quickly through our ports as they experience reduced processing times on arrival in the UK. This, with the use of the other measures detailed above, represents an integrated and flexible approach to border control.

Biometric Registration

6.15   Passenger clearance is extremely staff intensive and the Government is committed to technological solutions, not only to detect and deter clandestine entrants, but also to increase further the effectiveness of the control and the speed at which certain passengers will be able to pass through on their arrival in the UK. In order to achieve this we will develop an additional service for those in possession of a valid visa or leave to remain here or those who present a low risk to the immigration control or the security of the UK.

6.16   We will develop processes which allow entry to the UK to be automated by using biometrics technology, such as iris or facial recognition or fingerprints. Use of technology in this way will provide benefits for frequent travellers and those whose applications to travel here have already been accepted by virtue of their visa or leave to remain. The use of a biometric measure would also reduce the incidence of fraud, in that passports and/or UK visas held improperly would not be able to be used to gain entry because of the significantly enhanced security provided by unique biometric identifiers.

Scanners

6.17   The Government does not underestimate the enormity of the task of stemming the flow of people who enter the UK by concealing themselves in road and rail freight. The additional steps we must take to combat illegal migration were announced in Dover last September. We are investing heavily in new technology designed to detect persons concealed in vehicles or containers destined for the UK. Such technology includes:

- X/gamma ray scanners: purchased to be placed initially at Dover and Coquelles. We then intend to extend rapidly their availability at other points of entry. The Immigration Service is already sharing scanners owned by Customs & Excise.
- Heartbeat sensors: trials held at Dover and Coquelles of sensors which can detect, by its movement, the heartbeat of a person concealed within a stationary vehicle.
- Millimetric wave imaging equipment: Eurotunnel have been conducting trials with millimetric wave imaging equipment which they are using to good effect in Coquelles. We are following the trials with great interest and monitoring the effectiveness of the equipment which senses radiation emitted from within a vehicle.

Mobile Task Forces and an intelligence-led control

6.18   We live in an increasingly fast-paced world where we must act swiftly and flexibly, not only to provide the best possible service to our genuine customers but also to counter the actions of unscrupulous dealers in organised trafficking in humans. These criminal gangs have come to know and, as a result, exploit our immigration procedures. We are therefore committed to finding ways for the Immigration Service to operate less predictably, so that we might employ hard-hitting measures against these people. We believe that the efficient use of intelligence to target resources is fundamental to this approach. Recent legislation has extended powers for examining officers, normally police officers, to request information about passengers and goods on all journeys by ship and aircraft to, from and within the UK. This will be an important counter-terrorist tool and will be useful in providing information about the movements of other serious criminals such as people traffickers and drug smugglers.

6.19   In addition, the Immigration Service is forming specialist teams, consisting of highly trained
        officers. Acting on improved and more effective use of intelligence, these 'Mobile Task Forces'
        will be sent to targeted locations anywhere in the United Kingdom. An integrated intelligence
        network that supports the Mobile Task Forces will enable the Immigration Service to increase
        resources, for limited periods of time, on identified areas of greatest risk. As the risk changes,
        the Mobile Task Forces will be redeployed to focus on the new area of concern. The ability
        to plan and allocate resources in this way is key for the Immigration Service to maximise
        delivery in all areas of their business.

Co-operation

6.20   As well as strengthening border controls, the UK has an important interest in strengthening
        controls at the external borders of the EU and enhancing border controls as well as related
        infrastructure in transit countries. This will remain a major Government priority particularly in
        the period up to and following EU enlargement. In 1999-2000, the UK led a major EU project
        to enhance the management of the Polish eastern border working with France, Germany
        and the Netherlands. In 2002-2003, we shall be leading a similar project in Malta working
        with Spain. The Prime Minister's initiative in the Balkans (see Chapter 5) is tackling border
        controls on this important transit route. This will be complemented shortly by a UK led
        project working with Belgium, Turkey and the Czech Republic to enhance the asylum and
        immigration infrastructure in Bosnia. UK experts participate regularly in multi-country missions,
        led by the European Commission, to evaluate border controls and infrastructure arrangements
        in candidate countries to help target EU financial and other support and to inform negotiations
        on accession.

6.21   The difficulties caused by illegal immigration and in particular the problems caused by so
        many potential clandestine immigrants around Calais in northern France is an area in which
        we see the crucial importance of close co-operation with our colleagues in France. At the bi-
        annual UK/French summit in February 2001, we established a Cross-Channel Commission
        to allow closer bilateral discussion of cross-Channel issues, including illegal immigration.
        We are dealing with the problem of illegal immigration across the Channel jointly by increasing
        controls and law enforcement in the Calais area. In September 2001, the Home Secretary
        and the French Interior Minister agreed a number of practical measures designed to tighten
        controls at Channel ports and reduce the flow of would-be illegal immigrants into the Calais
        area. One of these measures involved sending more immigration officers to Coquelles. France
        also agreed to take tougher legal action against those who gain unauthorised access to the
        Eurotunnel site at Coquelles.

6.22   Close co-operation is key in the fight against those who seek to abuse the immigration control. While we enjoy good relations with our European counterparts, we have also concentrated on improving links between Government departments which share similar concerns. That is why we are encouraging the creation of Joint Intelligence Units, such as the one based in Folkestone, where the Immigration Service, Kent Police, HM Customs & Excise and the Benefits Agency work together, sharing intelligence and experience. In addition to the initiatives undertaken to develop Immigration Service expertise in the arrest of immigration offenders (set out in Chapter 4), we are also looking at the possibilities of the Immigration Service, Customs and ports police sharing accommodation at locations where this is feasible. In addition, we are exploring joint opportunities for training. All this will help to improve further our mutual understanding and expertise. The Government is committed to fostering this co-operation.

Chapter 7

MARRIAGE/FAMILY VISITS AND WAR CRIMINALS

Marriage

7.1   In June 1997, this Government abolished the 'primary purpose' rule which prevented foreign spouses coming to the United Kingdom where it was judged that the primary purpose of the marriage was admission to this country. We held it to be unfair and arbitrary as it caught not just bogus marriages, but also genuine arranged marriages where the parties intended to live together permanently in the UK. It was, though, accepted that among many ethnic groups there was a continuing desire for parents to choose someone of a similar cultural background as partners for their children. As time goes on, we expect the number of arranged marriages between UK children and those living abroad to decline. Instead, parents will seek to choose a suitable partner for their children from among their own communities in this country.

7.2   While embracing the diverse nature of our society, there are certain norms in relation to marriage in this country which we recognise as acceptable. For example, a marital partnership should be formed of only one man and only one woman – we do not recognise polygamous households. Neither will we tolerate forced marriages. A man or woman must be free to decide whether to enter into marriage.

7.3   Those entering into marriage must also be of an age where they are legally responsible adults with an understanding of the full implications of what they are doing and capable of making informed decisions about their own future. Currently, we do not permit entry clearance to be granted to those under 16 years of age on the basis of marriage. We should have the same prohibition in the Immigration Rules preventing those under 16 years of age from being granted entry clearance as fiancés.

7.4   There is a growing body of evidence that a greater proportion than was previously appreciated of people in the country and seeking leave to remain on the basis of marriage are not, in fact, in genuine relationships. In some cases, they will simply have 'duped' a person resident here into marriage, with the intention of leaving that person as soon as they have obtained settlement status. They may often then try to bring their genuine long-term partner into the country to join them here. In other cases, the person may have paid someone to go through a marriage ceremony with them or used an organised crime group, a corrupt solicitor or immigration adviser to arrange a bogus marriage for them. In its first year of operation, there were around 700 reports of suspicious marriages forwarded to the Immigration Service by Registrars. These are only the most obvious and blatant cases where the Registrar has strong evidence that the couple are not in a genuine relationship. There may be many other cases of bogus marriage not reported by Registrars. Reports of suspicious marriages can be followed up by an Immigration Service investigation or by interview and we are increasing the number of interviews carried out by caseworkers.

7.5   The Government intends to make it more difficult for those who seek leave to remain on the basis of a bogus marriage, while at the same time recognising changes in marital trends. We propose to:

- Increase the probationary period for leave to remain on the basis of marriage.
- Revise the Immigration Rules for unmarried partners.
- Simplify the procedures for genuine applicants.
- Consider revising the Immigration Rules to prevent switching into marriage.

INCREASING THE PROBATIONARY PERIOD

7.6   We intend to increase the probationary period on marriage so that a person will be given leave to remain for two years before they can apply for settlement. The couple will need to prove that, during the two-year period, they have been able to maintain and accommodate themselves without recourse to public funds. While this will not greatly inconvenience or penalise those in genuine relationships, it will provide a longer period to test the genuineness of the marriage and increase the chance of exposing sham marriages.

7.7   It would be harder to sustain a relationship for this longer period with a duped partner and it is more likely that, when questioned or interviewed, the lack of a genuine and subsisting relationship will become apparent.

UNMARRIED PARTNERS

7.8   With fewer people marrying, and an increase in applications for leave to enter or remain in the UK as unmarried partners, extending the probationary period on marriage to 2 years will also remove the current distinction between marriage cases and those of unmarried partners in relationships akin to marriage where the probationary period is already 2 years. We also intend to remove the requirement in the Immigration Rules that unmarried partners must be legally unable to marry before they can benefit from their relationship under the Rules.

SIMPLIFYING PROCEDURES

7.9   The guiding rule for granting leave to remain on the basis of either a marriage or partnership is that the relationship should be genuine and intended to be permanent. While concentrating effort on tackling bogus marriages, the Government is also considering whether we can simplify the current procedures where there is clear evidence that a genuine marriage exists. At present all those given entry clearance on the basis of marriage to a UK citizen, or person settled in the UK, are given leave to enter for 12 months to serve a probationary period before settlement is granted. This is the same whether the couple are newly married or have been married for some years but living abroad.

7.10   In cases of existing long-term relationships, the scrutiny of the marriage or relationship for a further period seems unnecessary. We therefore propose to remove the probationary period in those cases where the couple have been married or can show evidence of a genuine and subsisting cohabitative relationship, akin to marriage, for 5 years or more. Provided that the entry clearance officer is so satisfied, we propose that he should grant a settlement entry clearance at the outset. Such a provision would allow proper in-depth enquiries to be made at posts abroad. It would **only** be available to those seeking entry clearance from abroad and there would be no switching into this category after arrival in the UK. This should encourage those in a genuine long-term relationship to apply for entry clearance abroad. Applicants in the UK will have to serve the standard 2-year probationary period, along with those who are newly married and those whose unmarried partnership is of a shorter duration.

NO SWITCHING

7.11   We will also consider the introduction of a 'no switching' provision to prevent persons applying to remain on the basis of marriage after entering the UK in a different category. In 1999, 76% of those granted leave to remain on the basis of marriage had been admitted to the UK for another purpose and 50% of those who switched into the marriage category did so within 6 months of entry. As it seems unlikely that such a large percentage of this number would develop permanent relationships within such a short period of time, the indication is that many of these persons had intended to marry all along but had not obtained leave to enter on this basis and had therefore lied about their intentions to the entry clearance officer. Alternatively, they may have entered a bogus marriage to obtain leave to remain after arrival.

7.12   Although entry clearance is mandatory for those seeking entry to the UK on the basis of marriage, in practice some persons are presently allowed to switch into this category. This is unfair to those applicants who follow the correct procedures by applying for entry clearance overseas and pay for the appropriate visa.

7.13   In some cases, there may be many compassionate factors which would need to be taken into account before enforcing a person's removal to seek a marriage entry clearance abroad. Such factors may be particularly strong where the person has been living in the UK for some time and has formed extremely close links with this country and with his or her new family. There are likely to be fewer factors when the person has been in this country for only a short time.

Family visits

7.14   The Government understands the distress that can be caused in a small number of cases when a close family relative is refused a visa to attend a family event – in particular a funeral. Visa issuing posts overseas always make every effort to deal with genuine, urgent, compassionate cases with the utmost speed. But they must also be alert to those who may attempt to abuse our immigration controls in order to gain entry to the UK.

7.15   The idea of a financial bond scheme, whereby a relative in the UK could act as a financial guarantor in such cases, has been carefully considered. But it proved controversial and widely unpopular with ethnic minority communities and would have been very difficult to operate alongside a more flexible immigration control. We want an open and constructive debate on this issue and would welcome contributions. We may, for instance, need to explore community-based, or other collective, mechanisms or a way of requiring people to report back to posts when they return. Any solution will need to be quick and simple if it is genuinely going to help in this sort of case.

7.16   We re-introduced a right of appeal for family visitors in October 2000 to assist those whose application to visit the UK for a family event is unsuccessful. In January last year, we began a detailed review of this right of appeal. This review is nearing completion and we will publish the results shortly. We recognise that in circumstances such as the sudden and unexpected death of a relative it is not practicable to wait until an appeal is decided. But we need to take account of the findings of the research on family visitor appeals to ensure that the system is coherent and consistent. We shall examine the results of the review and assess what further work needs to be done to ensure that funeral visitors are given every chance to come to the UK.

War criminals

7.17   Crimes against humanity can be committed at any time and the international community regards these, and war crimes, as amongst the most serious crimes which can be committed. The Government is determined to ensure that those who are guilty of committing such atrocities are called to account for their actions wherever possible. In cases where criminal proceedings, either in the UK or abroad, are not practicable, the Government is intent on making more effective use of its immigration and nationality powers to prevent suspected war criminals from entering the country or from establishing themselves here.

7.18   Historically, the main focus in the UK has been the presence of alleged Nazi war criminals. These concerns led to the setting-up in 1988 of the War Crimes Inquiry and to the passing of the War Crimes Act 1991. This enabled the prosecution in UK courts of British citizens, or those resident here, who had committed acts of murder or manslaughter in German-occupied territory during the Second World War. The police continue to investigate allegations where there are sufficient grounds to do so, although with the passage of time the likelihood of further prosecutions is clearly becoming more remote.

7.19   In recent years, the international community has had to grapple with the consequences of new generations of war criminals, born out of the conflicts in the former Yugoslavia, Rwanda and elsewhere. The Government has strongly supported international efforts to bring the perpetrators of war crimes to justice through the establishment of ad hoc criminal tribunals and the International Criminal Court. The International Criminal Court Act 2001 also gives the UK jurisdiction to prosecute in its domestic courts both British citizens and others who are resident here even where they are suspected of having committed atrocities abroad. This jurisdiction applies only to events which occur after the date of its introduction (1 September 2001).

7.20   The UK should not provide a safe haven for war criminals or those who commit crimes against humanity. Action should be taken to bring such individuals to justice wherever possible within the rule of law and depending on the sufficiency of the evidence available. However, our experience, and that of a number of other countries which have been very active in this field, is that an effective response cannot be founded solely on criminal prosecution. Frequently, evidence will be insufficient to meet the high standard of proof required to convict a particular individual. Governments must be prepared to use their full range of powers, including the selective use of immigration and nationality provisions, to make it clear that those who are suspected of involvement in atrocities are not welcome in a civilized society. All of this needs to be balanced against our obligations to individuals who are in genuine need of protection.

7.21   The Government intends to strengthen its ability to deal with suspected and convicted war criminals by:

- Up-dating relevant immigration and nationality legislation.
- Ensuring better co-ordination between the Home Office and all the other Departments and agencies who have an interest in this area.

STRENGTHENING LEGISLATIVE POWERS

7.22   We will amend the Immigration Rules to make it clear that suspected war criminals can be refused entry to, and leave to remain in, the UK on the grounds of their conduct, character or associations.

7.23   We will also expand the role of the Special Immigration Appeals Commission (SIAC) so that, in addition to dealing with cases of suspected terrorists, the Commission will also be able to hear certain appeals against the refusal of leave in respect of alleged war criminals. The SIAC procedure is used only in exceptional circumstances and this change will involve only those cases where a refusal is based on sensitive information which cannot be disclosed publicly. In this way, the information can be suitably protected while enabling the grounds of appeal to be fully considered.

7.24   We will introduce a power to enable indefinite leave to enter or remain (ILE/R) to be revoked in cases where a suspected war criminal has gained that status by failing to disclose, when asked, a relevant fact such as information about their activities.

7.25   We will also amend the British Nationality Act 1981 so that action can be taken in appropriate cases to deprive a suspected war criminal of British citizenship. The proposed changes are described in more detail in paragraphs 2.22-2.23.

IMPROVED CO-ORDINATION

7.26   Because the response to war criminals must take account of the full range of the Government's powers it is essential that the various Departments and agencies involved act in a co-ordinated way. In the past, consideration of these issues has been fragmented. A framework for closer co-operation has already been established, improving communication amongst Departments when individual cases come to light. The Government wants now to focus on the contribution which the use of immigration and nationality powers might make in this area rather than continuing to rely on the use of criminal proceedings. The Government is establishing an inter-Departmental group whose task will be to build on progress made through closer co-operation, ensuring that there is an appreciation of the full range of possible responses and to develop further a more coherent Government-wide strategy to support the 'no safe haven' policy.

7.27   As other countries have found, dealing with war criminals is a highly complex and difficult business. Developing more effective arrangements here will involve time, expertise and substantial resources. The Government believes, however, that it is imperative that the UK should mark its abhorrence of war crimes by doing all it can to call the perpetrators to account, continuing to support the work of the international criminal tribunals and the International Criminal Court, and using its immigration and nationality powers where criminal proceedings are not possible.

Chapter 8

CONCLUSION

8.1   The challenges we face are immense and we will need to be flexible and proactive. Our standards of service, our welcome to those who need our protection and who can contribute to our society and our unequivocal messages of deterrence to those who break our laws and abuse our hospitality will remain under close scrutiny. We must recognise the high levels of interest in our work and ensure we live up to expectations.

8.2   Just some of the work that has already begun to pay dividends and the further measures we will take forward – through legislation where necessary – are summarised below:

What we have done already

- Speeded up the process of acquiring British citizenship.
- Developed exceptional service levels for the issue of work permits.
- Speeded up and increased the number of initial asylum decisions.
- Introduced a Highly Skilled Migrant Programme to enable the most talented migrants to come to the UK.
- Introduced an Innovator Scheme.
- Established the first Induction Centre for asylum seekers.
- Issued the first Application Registration Cards to asylum seekers.
- Agreed a Protocol with the police and used charter flights to increase the number of removals of failed asylum seekers.
- Tackled the criminals who traffic and smuggle through intelligence and enforcement operations which continue.
- Deployed airline liaison officers stationed overseas to prevent improperly documented passengers travelling to the UK.
- Placed immigration officers at French stations to check passengers before they travel here.
- Expanded the appeals system so the Immigration Appellate Authorities are now receiving 4,500 asylum appeals a month. This will rise to 6,000 from November this year.

What we are doing now

- Considering a more flexible approach to the residence requirements for naturalisation.
- Letting certain postgraduate students switch into employment by amending the Immigration Rules at an early opportunity.
- Meeting the demand for short-term casual labour building on the principles of the Seasonal Agricultural Workers' Scheme.
- Planning publication of a consultation document to review the Working Holidaymaker Scheme to make it more inclusive.
- Encouraging changes to ensure that Ministers of religion are in tune with and able to appreciate fully the environment in which they will be teaching and working.
- Further expanding our detention facilities to facilitate an increased number of removals.
- Better assisting unaccompanied asylum seeking children and sharing support for them across a wider number of local authorities while sifting out adults posing as children.
- Further developing our strategy for refugee integration by funding projects and leading the National Refugee Integration Forum to produce practical solutions.
- Combating illegal working by more effective enforcement action, less potential for fraud, effective gathering and sharing of information and working with business (legislation will be needed as part of this).
- Preventing people trafficking and smuggling in source and transit countries.
- Co-operating with our EU colleagues to tackle illegal immigration and strengthen the EU's common borders.
- Dealing appropriately with the victims of organised crime.
- Investing heavily in new technology to detect people concealed in vehicles or containers.
- Amending Immigration Rules to make clear the basis for refusing entry to war criminals.
- Proposing revision of the Immigration Rules to tackle bogus marriages, simplify the procedures in respect of genuine marriages and to remove the current distinctions between married and unmarried partners.
- Addressing our research and information requirements to inform further policy development.

What we need to introduce through legislation

Amongst other measures we will legislate to:

- Require applicants for naturalisation to demonstrate they have a certain standard of English.
- Allow a citizenship ceremony to be held as an integral part of the naturalisation process.
- Update our ability to deprive people of citizenship in those rare cases where it is appropriate.

- Update the nationality legislation.
- Introduce a power to charge for work permits to cover the cost of the excellent service.
- Regulate those who provide advice and services in respect of work permits.
- Develop a resettlement programme to let those most in need of protection come here legally.
- Introduce Accommodation Centres on a trial basis for asylum seekers with a total capacity of approximately 3000.
- Phase out voucher support.
- Streamline our appeals system to cut down delay and remove barriers to removal.
- Expand our programme of assisting those who want to return home to do so before their asylum claim is determined.
- Increase the penalty for facilitating illegal entry and harbouring to 14 years.
- Legislate on trafficking for labour and sexual exploitation including a new offence of trafficking for the purposes of sexual exploitation with a penalty of 14 years.
- Make provision for carriers to check the details of passengers when they book a ticket before travel.
- Introduce provisions to allow entry to the UK through technology such as iris or facial recognition.
- Introduce a power to revoke indefinite leave to remain in specified circumstances.

Annex A

Summary of naturalisation requirements and provisions in other countries, November 2001

	Australia	Austria	Canada	France	Germany	Netherlands	USA
1st Generation							
Min. Residence period?	Min. 1 of 2 years	6 years	3 of 4 years	5 years	8 years	5 years before applic.	5 years
Knowledge of society?	Yes	–	Yes	No, but integration must be demonstrated	–	Yes	Yes
Language skills?	Yes	Yes	Yes	Yes	Yes	Yes	Yes
Good character?	Yes	–	–	Yes	–	–	Yes
Absence of Criminal Record?	Yes	Yes	Yes	Yes	Yes	Yes	Possibly
Dual Cit. formally accepted?	Yes	No	Yes	Yes	No	No	No
Oath?	Yes	No	Yes	No	Yes	No	Yes
Language Classes							
Classes?	Yes	No	Yes	Proposed	Proposed	Yes	Yes
Compulsory attendance?	No	Yes	No	n.a.	Yes	Yes	No
Citizenship Classes							
Separate from lang. classes?	No	No	No		Yes	No	n.a.
Compulsory classes?	No	Yes	No		Yes	Yes	n.a.

Summary of naturalisation requirements and provisions in other countries, November 2001 (continued)

	Australia	Austria	Canada	France	Germany	Netherlands	USA
Citizenship Classes (continued)							
Areas covered?	History, culture, accessing public services	History, culture	History, culture, accessing public services		Legal order, culture and history	Culture and heritage, accessing public services	n.a.
Run by?	Local service providers – government funded	n.a.	Local service providers – government funded		n.a.	Local service providers – government funded	
Citizenship Ceremonies							
Provision?	Yes	Yes	Yes	Yes	No, but held in some towns	No	Yes
Compulsory Attendance?	Yes	No	Yes	No, but in practice, yes	No		Yes
Individual or group ceremony?	Group	Both	Group	Both	Group		Group
Certificate?	Yes	n.a.	Yes	Yes	Yes	Yes	Yes
Letter?	No	n.a.	No	Yes	No	No	No
Fees?	None	n.a.	None	None	None	None	None
Other form of recognition?	No	n.a.	No	n.a.	None	No	None

Source: Simon Green, 'Citizenship for migrants: a comparison of contexts and procedures in seven countries' report prepared for the Home Office (IRSS), November 2001

Annex B

PROPOSED CITIZENSHIP PLEDGE FOR PEOPLE BECOMING BRITISH CITIZENS

I [swear by Almighty God] [do solemnly and sincerely affirm] that, from this time forward, I will give my loyalty and allegiance to Her Majesty Queen Elizabeth the Second Her Heirs and Successors and to the United Kingdom. I will respect the rights and freedoms of the United Kingdom. I will uphold its democratic values. I will observe its laws faithfully and fulfil my duties and obligations as a British citizen.

Annex C1

Recruitment difficulties – Hard-to-fill vacancies by sector, Employers Skills Survey (ESS) 2001

	Agriculture	Manufacturing	Constructiion	Wholesale & Retail	Hotels & Restaurants	Transport & Comms	Finance	Business Services	Public Admin	Education
Total vacancies	10,714	77,110	39,562	124,934	59,146	50,982	28,471	185,963	26,946	30,764
Total hard-to-fill vacancies	7,687	35,246	23,601	50,624	25,983	22,505	8,436	94,813	7,910	14,189
Total skills shortages vacancies	1,146	21,443	15,438	18,516	5,881	7,215	4,253	51,749	2,729	5,314
Hard-to-fill vacancies due to skill shortages	15%	61%	65%	37%	23%	32%	50%	55%	35%	37%
Hard-to-fill vacancies not due to skill shortages	85%	39%	35%	63%	77%	68%	50%	45%	65%	63%

Source: Employers Skill Survey 2001 (IER/IFF)
Base: All establishments

Annex C2

International entry routes for high skilled migrants: Examples of how other countries are developing their migration routes to attract high skilled workers

USA	In 1990 the H-1B speciality (professional) workers visa was launched enabling highly skilled foreign workers to fill labour market shortages. In 2000 to further enable employers to compete internationally the annual quota of H-1B visas was raised from 65,000 per year in 1998 to 195,000 per year for 2000 to 2003. Other recent initiatives include enabling visa holders to switch employers as soon as a new employer files a petition on their behalf and 10,000 visas have been reserved to attract the best high tech students.
Canada	Canada has both temporary and permanent programmes for admitting highly skilled workers. The Canadian temporary worker programme introduced a software pilot, now de facto permanent, programme in 1997 to streamline the entry of those workers whose skills were in high demand in the software industry. In October 2001 it was announced that the programme would be extended to other industries such as engineering and construction.
	In November 2001 the spousal employment authorisation programme (introduced in 1998,) was made permanent. This allows the spouses of highly skilled temporary migrants to have immediate access to employment without a labour market test. The scheme aims to make Canada more attractive to foreign highly skilled workers and senior executives in key sectors of the economy.
Australia	Australia has well established points tested permanent and temporary skilled migration programmes. A skill-matching programme for potential permanent migrants has been designed to help overcome regional skills shortages. Details are stored on a database and this information is made available to employers and state and territory governments who may then nominate an applicant for migration. The business skills migration programme encourages successful business people to settle permanently in Australia and develop new business opportunities.
	The temporary business entry programme enables employers to sponsor and recruit staff from overseas for up to 4 years when they are unable to meet their skills need within the Australian labour market. 37,000 visas were issued in 2000-01. Educational visas enable educational and research institutions to recruit for positions that cannot be filled from the Australian labour market and grants of medical practitioner visas now have a much greater focus on providing service to rural and remote communities.
Denmark	Shortages in IT, biotechnology and medical occupations have resulted in a new fast-track work permit application scheme.
France	Due to a shortage of professionals working in science, research and IT, in 1998 a new fast-track work permit application process was introduced. Subject to certain criteria (evidence of qualification and/or an annual salary of over 180,000 Ffr), there is no labour market test. In 2000, 2,600 work permits were given to IT specialists.

International entry routes... (continued)

Germany	In 2000, the Federal Government introduced an 'IT specialists temporary relief programme' ('Green Card' scheme), making it possible for IT specialists to work in Germany for up to 5 years. The procedures are as rapid and transparent as possible. The quota was originally set at 10,000 rising to 20,000 according to further prevailing requirements. By November 2001, 10,415 Green card permits had been issued. Foreign students graduating with a German IT degree have immediate access to a work and residence permit.
	The programme is expected to provide an interim solution to IT skill shortages and it is anticipated that the domestic labour market will eventually meet labour demands. At the same time, a major vocational and continuing education initiative for German employees and young people has been introduced.
	In August 2001, the Government produced proposals for a new Immigration Bill. The proposals imply a major overhaul of the German immigration system – removing red tape, making it easier for certain categories of worker to obtain permanent residency, removing restrictions on access to the labour market for dependants, basing inflows on regional labour market needs, developing a new quota based entry route, and easier switching for graduates.
Ireland	In June 2000, the Irish Government introduced a fast-track working visa/work authorisation scheme to serve designated sectors of the employment market where skills shortages are particularly acute. Industries covered by the scheme include IT, construction professionals, engineers and nurses.
	Since 1999 intra-company transfers have been exempt from work permit requirements for a maximum period of 4 years. Also, students requiring visas who complete a course of education and secure employment in a related field are entitled to change their status and enter the work permit system without returning home. There are no restrictions on non-visa nationals moving from student to employee status, provided they obtain a work permit in order to do so.
Netherlands	Since 1995 a special tax allowance has been available to foreign workers posted with a domestic employer in the Netherlands, although in 2001 the tax-exempt allowance was reduced from 35 % to 30%.
	In 2001 a fast-track work permit procedure was introduced for applicants working in the IT sector. Employers can apply for a permit directly to the central office rather than to the regional office of the public employment service (this speeds up the procedure by about 2 weeks). Key personnel of multinational companies are exempted from labour market testing in order to reduce the red tape for foreign investors in the Netherlands.

Source: Based on work for the Home Office by the Migration Research Unit at University College London, examining the experiences of other countries in managing entry flows of highly skilled migrants for employment purposes.

In addition to those listed, other countries such as Italy, Sweden and Norway have initiated a review of their migration systems with the aim of bringing them more closely into line with the needs of local labour markets.

Annex D1

Work Permits

What is the duration of the visa/work permit?	Work Permits are issued for the duration requested by the employer, up to a maximum of five years.
Is the route quota restricted?	No.
What are the eligibility criteria?	a. Employers need to demonstrate they have a trading presence in the UK. b. There must be a genuine vacancy in the UK. c. The overseas national must be qualified and/or have experiences to NVQ level 3 or above. d. There must be no suitable resident workers available. e. The pay should be at least equal to those normally given for similar work. There are different requirements in the case of sportspeople and entertainers.
Are there any exemptions?	No.
Are any groups given facilitated access?	N/A
Is entry to the UK tied to a specific employer?	An employer must apply for a permit on behalf of the overseas national. However, the individual may change employers provided a new work permit application is approved.
Where can application forms be obtained?	From www.ind.homeoffice.gov.uk
Where are applications made?	An application is only acceptable if made by a British based employer who needs to employ a person.
What are the application procedures?	Applications, with the relevant supporting documents can be made by an employer both by post and by e-mail.
What is the consideration/ processing timescale?	Target of deciding 90% of complete applications within 1 day of receipt.
How are criteria confirmed and tested?	Applications are considered on the evidence provided through the application.
Are there possibilities for visa renewal?	Work permits can generally be extended by the completion of an extension application form and approved for up to a further 5 years.

Work Permits (continued)

Are there any possibilities for switching to other employers or from other entry routes?	Yes. When an individual is offered a post by a different employer, that employer must apply for a fresh work permit. It may also be possible for individuals to switch from other entry routes to work permit employment.
Are there any labour market restrictions?	Yes. An employer submitting a work permit application needs to show why they cannot fill the post with a resident worker, although this is waived for certain categories i.e. shortage occupatiuons.
Do spouses have access to labour market?	Dependants of work permit holders are permitted to take up employment as long as the permit holder remains in approved employment.
Are there any possibilities for family reunion?	Spouses and children under the age of 18 may join work permit holders in the UK, and take up employment here.
Can the route lead to permanent settlement?	Yes. After 4 years in employment, an application may be made for indefinite leave to remain in the UK.

Annex D2

Innovators

What is the duration of the visa/work permit?	18 Months. After the initial 18 months, a further 2 years can be obtained on an Innovators visa. Settlement can be applied for after the 4 years.
Is the route quota restricted?	No.
What are the eligibility criteria?	Assessment is on a points based system. Applicants must provide a business proposal that will lead directly to the creation of two full-time jobs within the business, within 12 months, for persons already in the UK. The applicant must be able to maintain and accommodate themselves in the UK for the initial 6 months without recourse to public funds, and must not take employment other than in their own business.
Are there any exemptions?	No.
Are any groups given facilitated access?	No.
Is entry to the UK tied to a specific employer?	No – Setting up own business
Where can application forms be obtained?	From www.ind.homeoffice.gov.uk, from diplomatic posts overseas and directly from the Immigration and Nationality Directorate.
Where are applications made?	Dependent on location of applicant.
What are the application procedures?	Submission of an application form, along with evidence.
What is the consideration/ processing timescale?	2 weeks from receipt in Business Case Unit.
How are criteria confirmed and tested?	By assessment of business plan submitted and verification of score given by applicant to business plan.
Are there possibilities for visa renewal?	Yes.
Are there any possibilities for switching to other employers or from other entry routes?	Yes - if in the UK in a legal capacity other than as a visitor.
Are there any labour market restrictions?	N/A – applicants will be establishing their own business.

Innovators (continued)

Do spouses have access to labour market?	Yes.
Are there any possibilities for family reunion?	Yes.
Can the route lead to permanent settlement?	Yes.

Annex D3

Highly Skilled Migrant Programme

What is the duration of the visa/work permit?	Initially one year. Further leave to remain in the UK will be granted where the applicant provides evidence of employment at a level warranted by the applicant's skill base.
Is the route quota restricted?	No.
What are the eligibility criteria?	Applicants need to score 75 points in 5 areas: educational qualifications, work experience, past earnings, achievement in chosen field and "priority applications".
Are there any exemptions?	Facilitated access for qualified doctors (see below).
Are any groups given facilitated access?	There will be a priority application concept to recruit qualified overseas doctors who wish to work as general practitioners in the UK.
Is entry to the UK tied to a specific employer?	No. The applicant does not require a work permit prior to being given leave to enter the UK.
Where can application forms be obtained?	From www.ind.homeoffice.gov.uk and from diplomatic posts abroad.
Where are applications made?	From overseas, but those who are in the UK in categories that lead to settlement can apply while still in the UK.
What are the application procedures?	Applicants will have to complete a form and supply evidence that they meet the criteria.
What is the consideration/ processing timescale?	Target of deciding 90% of applications (submitted with all relevant information) within one week of receipt.
How are criteria confirmed and tested?	By the evidence provided by the applicant.
Are there possibilities for visa renewal?	Yes, if evidence of employment at the appropriate skills level is provided (see above).
Are there any possibilities for switching to other employers or from other entry routes?	See "Where are applications made?".
Are there any labour market restrictions?	No.

Highly Skilled Migrant Programme (continued)

Do spouses have access to labour market?	Yes.
Are there any possibilities for family reunion?	Applicants may seek entry for their spouses and dependant children.
Can the route lead to permanent settlement?	As with existing non-temporary routes, migrants admitted under this scheme will be able to apply for settlement after they have been in the UK for 4 years.

Annex D4

Students switching into Work Permit Employment

What is the duration of the visa/work permit?	A work permit can be issued for any period up to 5 years, although settlement can be applied for after 4 years.
Is the route quota restricted?	No.
What are the eligibility criteria?	Students need to provide evidence that they: – have completed a recognised degree course at either a publicly-funded UK further or higher education institution or a recognised private education institution which maintains satisfactory records of enrolment and attendance; and – hold a valid work permit for employment; and – have written consent of any appropriate financial sponsor; and – do not have an adverse immigration history. Student nurses and postgraduate doctors and dentists need to provide evidence that they: – hold a vaild work permit for employment as a nurse, doctor or dentist; and – have written consent of any appropriate financial sponsor; and; – do not have an adverse immigration history.
Are there any exemptions?	No, although individual applications to switch into work permit employment from non-students will continue to be considered on an exceptional, discretionary basis.
Are any groups given facilitated access?	No.
Is entry to the UK tied to a specific employer?	Yes. A work permit must be obtained by the employer prior to the graduating student being permitted to switch.
Where can application forms be obtained?	www.ind.homeoffice.gov.uk.
Where are applications made?	An employer must obtain a work permit for the graduating student prior to taking up that employment. This will usually occur whilst the graduating student is still in the UK.
What are the application procedures?	See above.
What is the consideration/ processing timescale?	The same as for a normal work permit application.
How are criteria confirmed and tested?	By the evidence provided by the graduating student.

Students switching into Work Permit Employment

(continued)

Are there possibilities for visa renewal?	Yes.
Are there any possibilities for switching to other employers or from other entry routes?	N/A
Are there any labour market restrictions?	Student nurses and postgraduate doctors and dentists wishing to switch into employment must first obtain a work permit for employment as a nurse, doctor or dentist. For other graduating students, the same restrictions apply as to those applying for a work permit from abroad.
Do spouses have access to labour market?	Yes – same as for a normal work permit application.
Are there any possibilities for family reunion?	Yes – same as for a normal work permit application.
Can the route lead to permanent settlement?	Yes. After 4 years' work permit employment in the UK, an individual can apply for settlement.

Annex D5

Seasonal Agricultural Workers' Scheme

What is the duration of the visa/work permit?	The scheme runs from 1 May to 30 November. No work permits are required but participants must hold a work card issued by one of the 7 approved operators who administer the scheme on behalf of the Home Office. Visa nationals must also apply for a visa from their nearest British Mission.
Is the route quota restricted?	Yes, there is an annual quota, which currently stands at 15,200.
What are the eligibility criteria?	Applicants must be students in full-time education and aged 18-25.
Are there any exemptions?	No.
Are any groups given facilitated access?	No.
Is entry to the UK tied to a specific employer?	Yes, applicants must hold a work card issued by one of the operators of the scheme. This card will specify the farm to which the student has been allocated.
Where can application forms be obtained?	Work cards are obtained by applying to one of the scheme operators. Entry clearance application forms can be obtained from the applicant's nearest British Mission or from www.ind.homeoffice.gov.uk.
Where are applications made?	Applications for work cards and/or visas should be made in the applicant's home country.
What are the application procedures?	The scheme operators handle the recruitment process in its entirety. For those who also need a visa, they should apply at their nearest British Mission.
What is the consideration/ processing timescale?	This varies but may take several weeks.
How are criteria confirmed and tested?	Scheme operators liase directly with the applicant's university to check that they are genuine students. Entry clearance officers will also check the authenticity of documentation produced.
Are there possibilities for visa renewal?	Applicants should be granted leave to enter until 30 November of the year in question. If not they may apply to extend to this date as long as there is still work available for them.
Are there any possibilities for switching to other employers or from other entry routes?	Students are allocated to specific farms. Scheme operators may move them to another farm if work runs out. Those already in the UK in some other capacity may not switch into this category.

Seasonal Agricultural Workers' Scheme (continued)

Are there any labour market restrictions?	Yes, they are only permitted to take employment under the auspices of the scheme.
Do spouses have access to labour market?	No.
Are there any possibilities for family reunion?	Yes, dependants may apply for entry to the UK as visitors but will be bound by rules of entry for those visiting the UK.
Can the route lead to permanent settlement?	No.

Annex D6

Working Holidaymakers' Scheme

What is the duration of the visa?	The scheme allows Commonwealth citizens aged 17-27 to come to the UK for a maximum of 2 years. They may fund their holiday by working in the UK, provided such employment is incidental to the holiday. Incidental work means full-time employment (more than 25 hours a week) for 50% of the stay or less. Part-time work for a longer period is also permitted.
Is the route quota restricted?	No.
What are the eligibility criteria?	The scheme is only for Commonwealth citizens, aged 17-27. A working holidaymaker must be single, widowed or divorced. An applicant who is married can only qualify if they and their spouse intend coming to the UK on a working holiday together and both qualify in their own right. A working holidaymaker must not have any dependant children who will be 5 years of age or over during any part of the working holiday. Working holidaymakers must have the means to support themselves without recourse to public funds for at least the first 2 months after arrival. A prospective applicant must also intend to leave the UK on completion of their holiday.
Are there any exemptions?	No, but the UK also has a separate, bilateral youth exchange scheme with Japan.
Are any groups given facilitated access?	No.
Is entry to the UK tied to a specific employer?	No.
Where can application forms be obtained?	www.ind.homeoffice.gov.uk and at diplomatic posts abroad.
Where are applications made?	Applications must be made to diplomatic posts abroad.
What arc thc application procedures?	See above.
What is the consideration/ processing timescale?	Varies from post to post.
How are criteria confirmed and tested?	Entry clearance officers check that an individual meets the necessary criteria to qualify to enter the UK as a working holidaymaker.
Are there possibilities for visa renewal?	No. Only one working holidaymaker visa is permitted during the life of an individual.

Working Holidaymakers' Scheme (continued)

Are there any possibilities for switching to other employers or from other entry routes?	Working holidaymakers can switch between employers, and there are certain immigration categories, such as visitors, that they can switch into once in the UK.
Are there any labour market restrictions?	Yes. A working holidaymaker should not take up managerial positions or act as a locum hospital doctor, GP, solicitor or barrister. Some professional activity is allowed, such as supply teaching at a junior level, agency nursing, working as an occupational therapist, physiotherapist, speech therapist or radiographer.
Do spouses have access to labour market?	No, unless they enter the UK on a working holidaymaker visa (see "What are the eligibility criteria?").
Are there any possibilities for family reunion?	No.
Can the route lead to permanent settlement?	No.

Annex D7

Ministers of Religion

What is the duration of the visa?	Normally granted leave to enter the UK for 12 months initially. May apply for further extensions.
Is the route quota restricted?	No.
What are the eligibility criteria?	(i) Must have worked for 1 year as a minister of religion **or** if ordination is required by a faith in order to enter into ministry, must have been ordained as a minister of religion following 1 years full-time or 2 years part-time training; (ii) Must intend to work full-time.
Are there any exemptions?	No – the Rules apply to all faiths.
Are any groups given facilitated access?	No.
Is entry to the UK tied to a specific employer?	Yes, applicants apply to join a named religious establishment.
Where can application forms be obtained?	Entry clearance application forms can be obtained at the applicant's nearest British Mission offering an entry clearance service.
Where are applications made?	Applications should be made at the British Mission aboard.
What are the application procedures?	The completed entry clearance form should be submitted to the British Mission. Applicants may be required to attend an interview.
What is the consideration/ processing timescale?	This will vary from Mission to Mission.
How are criteria confirmed and tested?	Verification of documents provided to confirm applicant's status as a minister of religion. Verification that the host organisation in the UK is a recognised organisation.
Are there possibilities for visa renewal?	Yes, after 12 months applicants may apply to extend their stay. They may be granted an extension of up to 3 years at this stage.
Are there any possibilities for switching to other employers or from other entry routes?	Applicants may switch to another employer as long as they continue to meet the other requirements of the Immigration Rules. Those here in another capacity may apply to switch into this category - each case will be considered on individual merit.

Ministers of Religion (continued)

Are there any labour market restrictions?	Yes, may only take employment as a minister of religion.
Do spouses have access to labour market?	Yes.
Are there any possibilities for family reunion?	The applicant's spouse and dependant children may join them in the UK.
Can the route lead to permanent settlement?	Yes, after 4 years in continuous employment as a minister of religion, applicants may apply for permanent residency.

* The table refers only to those coming here as ministers of religion. In practice the category also caters for missionaries and those coming here as members of religious orders.

Annex E

REFUGEE RESETTLEMENT PROGRAMME

Existing arrangements

1   The UK currently operates two informal schemes to enable refugees to resettle in the UK: the mandate refugee scheme, and Ten or More plan[23]. We want to extend these programmes to increase the durable solutions available to those refugees whose protection cannot be safeguarded in their current place of refuge.

2   This type of larger resettlement scheme is well established in many countries:

Country	1999	2000	Year established
Denmark	500	500	1989
Netherlands	500	500	1984
Finland		700	1979
New Zealand	750	750	1979
Norway	1,480	1,481	Not known
Sweden	1,840	1,840	1950
Australia	8,000	8,000	1947
Canada	11,000	11,000	1978
USA	85,006	73,000	1980

3   We are currently working to develop the detail of what a resettlement programme to the UK will look like, and we are seeking the views and experience of refugee organisations in the course of determining this.

23 The mandate refugee scheme is available to those in need of resettlement who have settled family members in the UK who can support them until such time as they have permanent residence here. The Ten or More Plan provides resettlement to refugees with serious medical needs that cannot be provided in their initial place or refuge.

Before arrival in the UK

4   Each year the UNHCR[24] assesses the global need for resettlement. For the UK scheme, we envisage that UNHCR will assess where the need arises most acutely and whether there are particular nationalities or social groups for whom a resettlement need is high. This assessment, combined with our assessment of the UK's reception capacity, will be taken into account in deciding the UK resettlement programme and priorities for the coming year.

5   Under existing schemes operated by other resettlement countries, UNHCR, in assessing more general needs of those people in receipt of protection from them, also assess their need for resettlement[25]. If UNHCR considers that resettlement is necessary, their field officers will determine which country may be most appropriate for their resettlement. Papers are then passed to the Receiving State for their consideration, and the candidate is interviewed in order fully to understand their needs and situation. In many countries, security and health screening is also conducted.

6   When a candidate and his or her family is accepted for resettlement, they are counselled about what life will be like in their country of resettlement and the Receiving State prepares for their arrival (by issuing entry clearance/travel documentation, arranging accommodation, etc).

On arrival

7   Those families and individuals who are resettled to the UK will have additional needs to people who have claimed asylum in the UK. They will not have been through the process of induction, or provided with NASS support and they may have arrived with few or no possessions, or without suitable clothing for our climate. On arrival, therefore, assistance will be provided to ensure that their settlement in the UK is successful. This is likely to include the provision of temporary accommodation, counselling, advice on how to access services like education and health, and essential items for their day-to-day living.

8   We envisage that this assistance on arrival will be provided by a range of organisations, but funded by the Home Office.

---

24 United Nations High Commissioner for Refugees

25 Those in need of resettlement are those 'whose life, liberty, safety, health or other fundamental human rights are at risk in the country where they sought refuge'. For further information, sec the UNHCR's website: www.unhcr.ch

9   In drawing up the UK scheme we will be seeking to benefit from the experience of other countries and the UNHCR in respect of these and other aspects of the operation of resettlement programmes.

Annex F

Country Assessments

1   To inform decision-making on asylum applications by Home Office caseworkers and other officials involved in the asylum determination process, the *Country Information & Policy Unit (CIPU)* of the *Home Office Asylum and Appeals Policy Directorate* produce assessments on the countries that generate the largest number of asylum applications in the UK. These country assessments are published on the Home Office website. By their nature each country assessment concentrates on the main issues that are most likely to arise in the asylum determination process. The information contained in these country assessments is not exhaustive, nor does it catalogue all human rights violations. They are compiled from a wide variety of independent, reliable and well recognised sources that are listed at the end of each country assessment. They record factual information reported by other organisations.

2   Country Assessments are produced and published at six-monthly intervals – in practice this is done in April and October. Where key events occur between the 6 monthly publications, caseworkers are informed of changes in country conditions by means of Bulletins. We hope to be able to publish Bulletins on the Home Office website shortly.

3   The quality of assessments and the source information is being continuously, improved. In 2001 a research project was commissioned to evaluate the content and use of the country information. That research will be published. Some external stakeholders have suggested the establishment of an independent Documentation Centre, funded by, but independent of, Government, to undertake the production of country of origin information. This will be examined as part of the work that will be needed to follow up the findings of the research study mentioned above.

Annex G

Supporting information and research requirements

1. This White Paper sets out a forward looking strategy for our migration and asylum policies which is designed to respond to the challenges and opportunities of our global environment. It is crucial that these measures are accompanied by robust management information systems, and by high quality statistical, economic and social research. This will ensure that we can identify where our policies are working, what the economic and social impacts are, and where they could be improved. It will also help us to anticipate and respond to a rapidly changing environment.

2. Recognising the previous lack of research on migration, a major programme of research on immigration and asylum was established following the 1998 White Paper and 1999 Immigration & Asylum Act 1999. The programme was further extended following the publication by the Home Office of the research study 'Migration and Economic and Social Analysis' (RDS Occasional Paper No 67). This study, undertaken with help from the Performance and Innovation Unit in the Cabinet Office and the Institute of Public Policy Research, pulled together the existing theory and evidence on the economic and social impacts of migration. One of its conclusions was that our knowledge of the effects of migration is incomplete and that there are a number of areas that would benefit from further research. A further extensive cross-Departmental research programme was initiated. All this work has helped to inform the policies in this White Paper and a large number of reports are due to be published during the course of this year.[26]

3. The main requirements for information are now as follows:

---

26 There are links to published Home Office research studies on the Research, Development and Statistics website: www.homeoffice.gov.uk/rds/index.html

Citizenship and Nationality

4   For planning and monitoring purposes, it will be necessary to improve our analysis and forecasting of the volume of intake; and to conduct research into the effectiveness of the new procedures for English language acquisition on the integration of migrants and improving their contribution to society. Research findings from the 2001 Home Office Citizenship Survey (to be published later this year) will provide valuable contextual information about the general resident population and what they regard as the rights and responsibilities of UK residents as well as questions about identity. This information will separately distinguish the ethnic minorities (based on a large sub sample). The findings of the Citizenship Survey will help to inform the debate about citizenship and its implications for new migrants.

Working in the UK

5   A substantial amount of work has been undertaken using existing UK sources and analysis of international experience and research findings. The research has included:

- An assessment of the labour market outcomes of previous migrants to the UK and of the labour market impacts on the existing population.
- Analysis of the fiscal effects of migrants.
- Supporting information on the flows of migrants into and out of the UK and the composition of the current population of migrants in the UK.
- Research into the immigration control procedures used to manage the flows of migrants in such countries as Germany, Canada and the USA.
- Collaborative research with the Department for Work and Pensions to identify skill shortage vacancies and recruitment difficulties.
- Joint Home Office and Department for Trade and Industry research into push and pull factors.
- Research into the impact of migration on source countries, in particular on developing countries.

6   An important area for further research relates to the social effects of migration, particularly in the local areas where migrants settle. Some research has been undertaken on the impact of dispersal for local services and on the experiences of asylum seekers themselves. Further research under consideration includes a wider study of the local area impacts of migration, in conjunction with the Department for Transport, Local Government and the Regions, and the development of conceptual and statistical methods for monitoring the integration of refugees and other migrants.

Asylum

7   There are a number of elements under this heading:

   • A large area of research concerns the evaluation and improvement of the asylum processes for Induction Centres, Accommodation Centres, resettlement programmes, Reporting Centres, Removal Centres and the process of removals, as well as the associated appeal process. Monitoring systems are being devised to produce the management information and official statistics required and research will be commissioned to evaluate selected developments.

   • Evidence has been gathered from abroad on a number of these topics and this will be further extended to improve the implementation of the plans in this paper.

   • Research will continue on the evaluation and improvement of the refugee integration programmes under the Challenge Fund and the European Refugee Fund.

   • In addition some further research is being considered to gain a better understanding of the factors affecting asylum seekers' decisions including the sources of information on which they rely.

Tackling Fraud – People trafficking, illegal entry and illegal working

8   There are major gaps in our knowledge concerning the size, characteristics and impact of persons who are illegally resident and working in the UK. We will be considering ways of improving our information in this area. This is an area where collaboration across Government Departments and with non-Governmental Organisations will have an important contribution.

Contextual information

9   There is an important requirement to understand better the nature of international migration, including asylum seeking and illegal flows, and the factors and motivations influencing decisions to migrate. We plan to make full use of the international data and to exploit UK sources as far as possible. Unfortunately, relatively few of the existing data sources, including those concerned with service provision, identify recent migrants directly or by route of entry: we will be investigating the possibility of improving such sources.

10   The academic sector has an important role to play in developing our evidence base. In addition to UK-based researchers, the international research community is a valuable source of information and a potential partner for comparative research. In Canada and Australia, the Government has funded University centres of migration research. We will develop further our contacts and continue to engage external researchers so as to encourage their activity in policy related research. In addition, the Economic and Social Research Council is considering finding a longer term research programme on Population, Mobility and Movement which will help to promote research in this area.

11   This is an on-going programme of statistics, evaluation and research, and thereby an on-going process of refining and improving our policy. We will continue to develop our knowledge base and policy evaluation, feeding it directly into policy management, in order to ensure that we have an effective, forward looking nationality, asylum and immigration system.

Printed in the UK for The Stationery Office Limited
On behalf of the Controller of Her Majesty's Stationery Office.
84850 02/02